Climate Change
and
Natural Disasters

Climate Change
and
Natural Disasters

Transforming Economies and Policies for a Sustainable Future

Vinod Thomas

First published 2017

ISBN: 978-1-4128-6440-4 (hbk)
ISBN: 978-1-138-56735-1 (pbk)

Routledge
Taylor & Francis Group
LONDON AND NEW YORK

First published 2017 by Transaction Publishers

2 Park Square, Milton Park, Abingdon, Oxfordshire OX14 4RN
711 Third Avenue, New York, NY 10017

Routledge is an imprint of the Taylor & Francis Group, an informa business

First issued in paperback 2017

Library of Congress Catalog Number: 2016027013
ISBN-13: 978-1-4128-6440-4 (hbk)

Library of Congress Cataloging-in-Publication Data

Names: Thomas, Vinod, 1949- author.
Title: Climate change and natural disasters : transforming economies
    and policies for a sustainable future / Vinod Thomas.
Description: New Brunswick (U.S.A.) : Transaction Publishers, [2016] |
    Includes bibliographical references and index.
Identifiers: LCCN 2016027013 (print) | LCCN 2016027708 (ebook) |
    ISBN 9781412864404 (hardcover) | ISBN 9781412864527 (eBook) |
    ISBN 9781412864527
Subjects: LCSH: Climate change mitigation--Economic aspects. |
    Climatic changes--Economic aspects. | Natural disasters--Economic
    aspects. | Environmental economics. | Sustainable development.
Classification: LCC QC903 .T488 2016 (print) | LCC QC903 (ebook) |
    DDC 363.738/747--dc23
LC record available at https://lccn.loc.gov/2016027013

ISBN13: 978-1-4128-6440-4 (hbk)
ISBN13: 978-1-138-56735-1 (pbk)

To Dear Tejin
Who inspired our concern for nature

Contents

List of Figures

List of Tables

List of Boxes

Acknowledgments

I would like to thank Rajesh Pradhan, Ruth Francisco, Alice Martha Lee, and Marianne Juco for their special contribution at various stages of the writing of the book. Special thanks go to Erich Vogt, John Hay, Mohan Munasinghe, and Neil Britton for peer reviewing the manuscript.

My sincerest appreciation goes to the team leaders, staff, and the management team at the Asian Development Bank's Independent Evaluation Department. I am grateful for their generous support, advice, and inputs during the various phases of preparing the manuscript. Valuable comments from the following individuals are acknowledged: Ari Perdana, Kapil Thukral, Tomoo Ueda, Andrew Brubaker, Jiro Tominaga, Hans van Rijn, Walter Kolkma, Bob Finlayson, Joey Tan, and Garret Kilroy. I also gratefully acknowledge Gillian Morzal and Michael Diza for support.

I also wish to thank Satinder Bindra and his team at the Department of External Relations for the valuable comments and suggestions, as well as, editorial and publication support.

Foreword

The drive for economic growth, especially in Asia, brought striking economic gains over the past half a century. That progress came at a heavy cost in the form of environmental degradation as well as income disparities, raising concerns over the sustainability of the past pattern of growth. Facing an economic downturn today, policymakers would like to regain the growth momentum, but there is an emerging realization that future growth needs to be different and of better quality.

Climate change is the greatest price society is paying for decades of environmental neglect. The impact of global warming is most visible in the rising threat of climate-related natural disasters. Hazards of nature have always been with us, but the growing incidence of floods, storms, and droughts all across the world is putting a spotlight on the need for action. As this book argues, it will be harder to sustain growth unless the worst effects of climate change, notably natural calamities, are averted. Sustainability, understood as meeting the needs of the present without endangering future generations, is key to these efforts. Today, as countries grapple with the perils of climate change, sustainability has come to encompass a more mutually dependent set of environmental, economic, and social goals.

The book's focus on climate change and natural disasters is timely. The Third United Nations World Conference on Disaster Risk Reduction in 2015 in Japan set out the Sendai Framework for disaster risk reduction for 2015–2030. Global initiatives are backing a new development agenda for the next fifteen years with the launch of the Sustainable Development Goals by member countries of the United Nations. After decades of disappointment, action on climate change is gaining momentum and traction, with a global deal on emissions adopted at the 21st Conference of the Parties of the United Nations Framework Convention on Climate Change in December 2015.

Averting the worst effects of climate change is a big part of that agenda. We need to recognize the rising threat of hazards of nature and build in prevention into development programs. Turning aspiration for climate action and disaster prevention will require considerable resources and political will. Dealing with environmental deterioration and climate change as well as social inequities is not an impediment, but rather an aid, to economic growth. In fact going forward, it is the only way we can have lasting growth. Governments, businesses, civil society, and international institutions have a key role to play in supporting policies and investments for more sustainable growth.

Takehiko Nakao
President, Asian Development Bank

Preface

The first half of the 2010s will be remembered for deadly climate-related disasters. Among them the great floods in Thailand in 2011, Hurricane Sandy in the United States in 2012, and Typhoon Haiyan in the Philippines in 2013. Notably, it is hydrometeorological (floods, storms, heatwaves) and climatological (droughts, wildfires) disasters that are increasing, and not geophysical ones (earthquakes, volcanic eruptions). Floods and storms displace the most people. In 2014, 17.5 million people were displaced by climate-related disasters, ten times more than the 1.7 million displaced by geophysical hazards.

The surge of intense floods, storms, droughts, and heatwaves has an ominous link to climate change. Global temperatures have been steadily on the rise and 2015 was the hottest year since records began in 1880. Attention to climate-related disasters, arguably the most tangible manifestation of global warming, could help mobilize broader climate action. It could also be instrumental in transitioning to a path of low-carbon, green growth.

This book builds on the emerging relation between the growing threat of natural disasters and climate change, and its anthropogenic causes. There is a great divide between the scientific knowledge about the climate–disaster link on the one side, and analysis and policy on the other. Progress is predicated not just on knowing more about climate change but confronting the roadblocks to action.

Drawing from the dynamics of natural disasters and climate change, the book sends three messages.

- First, human-made factors are exerting a growing influence on natural phenomena. Natural disasters, especially climate-related disasters, are becoming increasingly anthropogenic events, with human actions influencing not only exposure and vulnerability, but also the nature of the hazards themselves.

- Second, because of the link to anthropogenic factors, there is a pressing need for climate mitigation. As it relates to disasters, such risk reduction measures are highly beneficial economically and socially. Disaster response is vital, but prevention to limit, if not avoid losses, needs to be the first step.
- Third, prevention, including climate mitigation, ought not to be viewed as a cost to economic growth but an investment. In fact, growth cannot be projected to continue without integrating climate impact and actions into the growth scenario. Shifting to a low-carbon growth trajectory is essential.

Taken together, the various strands requires a look at the process of economic growth more holistically; that is, not just as the result of the accumulation of physical capital and human capital, but also of natural capital. Doing so will not jeopardize growth but will lead to better and more lasting growth.

The book begins in the first chapter with the picture of rising natural disasters with climate change as a game changer. Chapter 2 then focuses on the nature of climate-related disasters and presents a framework that brings out human and economic factors that help influence hazards along with people's exposure and vulnerability. The next chapter examines the nature and trends of these climate-related disasters at the global and regional levels.

The rest of the book is about what needs to be done differently going forward. Chapter 4 takes up climate change mitigation and discusses measures like carbon pricing, energy subsidies, renewable energy, energy efficiency and building urban resilience. Chapter 5 concentrates on adaptation and disaster management in relation to climate change.

Many of the needed actions are not new, and their technical aspects are well understood. Chapter 6 stresses the role of political motivation and behavioral change in driving the desired transformation. The book concludes by offering a development paradigm that would confront climate change as part of the development agenda.

Abbreviations

ADB	Asian Development Bank
AfDB	African Development Bank
BNEF	Bloomberg New Energy Finance
CFCs	chlorofluorocarbons
CIFOR	Center for International Forestry Research
CO_2	carbon dioxide
COP21	21st Conference of Parties
CRED	Center for Research on Epidemiology of Disasters
DRLA	Disaster Resilience Leadership Academy
DRR	disaster risk reduction
EBRD	European Bank for Reconstruction and Development
ECG	Evaluation Cooperation Group
EDF	Électricité de France
EM-DAT	Emergency Events Database
G20	Group of Twenty
GDP	gross domestic product
GFDRR	Global Facility for Disaster Risk Reduction and Recovery
GHG	greenhouse gas
HCFCs	hydrochlorofluorocarbons
HFCs	hydrofluorocarbons
IDMC	Internal Displacement Monitoring Centre
IEA	International Energy Agency
IED	Independent Evaluation Department
IEG	Independent Evaluation Group
IFRC	International Federation of Red Cross and Red Crescent Societies
IMF	International Monetary Fund
IPCC	Intergovernmental Panel on Climate Change
JMA	Japan Meteorological Agency

NASA	National Aeronautics and Space Administration
NEDA	National Economic and Development Authority
NOAA	National Oceanic and Atmospheric Administration
OECD	Organisation for Economic Co-operation and Development
PAGASA	Philippine Atmospheric, Geophysical and Astronomical Services Administration
PM10	particulate matter of ten microns
ppm	parts per million
PSA	Philippine Statistics Authority
PSI	Pollutant Standard Indices
REDD+	Reduced Emissions from Deforestation and Degradation
RTCC	Responding to Climate Change
TMD	Thai Meteorological Department
UN	United Nations
UNDESA	United Nations Department of Economic and Social Affairs
UNEPGEAS	United Nations Environment Programme Global Environmental Alert Service
UNESCAP	United Nations Economic and Social Commission for Asia and the Pacific
UNFCCC	United Nations Framework Convention on Climate Change
UNISDR	United Nations Office for Disaster Risk Reduction
UNU-EHS	United Nations University-Institute for Environment and Human Security
US EIA	United States Energy Information Administration
WEF	World Economic Forum
WHO	World Health Organization
WMO	World Meteorological Organization

Endorsements

"*Climate Change and Natural Disasters* is not only a valuable survey of the causes and consequences of climate change, but also a ringing endorsement of the urgent need to incorporate disaster risk reduction in core economic planning alongside efforts to radically reduce greenhouse gas emissions."

—Robert Glasser, special representative of the
Secretary-General for Disaster Risk Reduction,
The United Nations Office for Disaster Risk Reduction

"A highly authoritative, lucid and timely analysis of the implications of climate change and disasters for sustainable development—the universally accepted path for humanity in the 21st century."

—Mohan Munasinghe, chairman,
Munasinghe Institute for Development

"A thought-provoking examination of the links between climate change and natural disasters, and how to tackle both. Its call for greater investments in natural capital, "nature's infrastructure"—in addition to physical and human capital—to meet these critical 21st century challenges is particularly timely and welcome."

—Inger Andersen, director general,
International Union for Conservation of Nature

"This excellent analysis confirms that in an increasingly fragile world we need greater focus on investment in disaster risk reduction, climate mitigation and adaptation. This is the only way to move towards the new paradigm we have universally endorsed with the Sustainable Development Goals."

—Kristalina Georgieva, European Commission
vice-president and former EU commissioner
for International Cooperation,
Humanitarian Aid and Crisis Response

"Recent extreme climate impacts in Asia and across the world under-score the urgent need to act on climate change. Policymakers need every resource available to put in place effective policies and incentives to achieve the vision outlined in the 2015 Paris Agreement, and this book holds great potential to secure the practical pathways that can turn the Paris vision into reality."

—Christiana Figueres, executive secretary,
United Nations Framework Convention
on Climate Change

"Estimates suggest that South and South-East Asia, as well as Sub-Saharan Africa, would be most severely affected by climate change, particularly by the increase in natural disasters. This new book provides an extensive survey of the issues of climate risk mitigation, adaptation, resilient infrastructure and calls for the transformation of policy framework. I highly welcome this input to address these long-term but imminent challenges."

—Rintaro Tamaki, deputy secretary-general,
Organisation for Economic Co-operation
and Development (OECD)

"This landmark study demonstrates that natural disasters are increasingly man-made. Cutting across knowledge domains it offers a comprehensive, positive and realistic policy agenda that captures the universal aspirations of the post 2015 sustainable development era."

—Robert Picciotto, former director general,
Independent Evaluation Group, World Bank

"This is a timely and engagingly written book on an important topic of increasing international concern."

—Jagdish Bhagwati, Columbia University

"By focusing on the connection between hazards of nature and climate change, this book provides compelling reasons for countries to switch urgently to a low-carbon growth path. This would enable the world not only to avoid the most damaging of the climate scenarios but would also deliver cities where we can move, breathe and be productive, investments to promote sustainable agriculture and rural economies, and foster ecosystems that can move from fragile to flourishing. A timely and essential read."

—Nicholas Stern, IG Patel Professor of
Economics and Government,
LSE and president, British Academy

"A compelling evidence-based call to action on the climate-natural disaster link. A must-read for development economists and advocates in rich and poor countries alike."

—Nancy Birdsall, president,
Center for Global Development

"The book provides rich data behind the realities Oxfam is grappling with every day—an escalation of disasters linked to climate change which are hitting the poorest hardest everywhere. Its call to radically scale-up investment in adaptation and building resilience must be heard if we are to tackle this climate injustice."

—Winnie Byanyima, executive director,
Oxfam International

1

Overview

We may utilize the gifts of nature just as we choose, but in her books the debits are always equal to the credits.
—Mahatma Gandhi

The severity and frequency of natural disasters are rising and have, in recent years, exacted a shocking toll in human and economic losses.[1] Disasters that caught international attention included the floods in Pakistan in 2010 that killed almost two thousand people and affected 20 million people. The floods submerged a fifth of the country in this once in a thousand years phenomenon. The heat wave in India in 2015 that saw temperatures averaging 40°C killed 2,400 people.

Hazards hitting densely populated areas are now more likely to turn into disasters by the sheer number of people exposed. By 2050, two-thirds of the world's population are expected to live in cities. While Asia remains mostly rural, with fewer than half of the population living in cities in 2014, the region is projected to urbanize rapidly in the coming years. Asia now has 16 of the world's twenty-eight megacities (cities with populations of over 10 million) including the three largest: Delhi, Shanghai, and Tokyo. These three, together with Dhaka and Kolkata, are also among the world's top ten most populous cities with the highest risk of flooding.

Typhoon Ketsana in September 2009—which dumped more rain on Manila in a matter of hours than would have been normal in a month for that time of year—was a particularly terrifying example of an extreme hydrometeorological event hitting a city (figure 1.1). In January 2014, Jakarta was also hit with pounding rains that brought the city to a standstill.

The economic damage from weather-related events since the 2010s can be eye-watering. The floods that submerged Thailand's industrial heartland in 2011 stopped production in computer and car factories,

1

Figure 1.1. Manila floods from Typhoon Ketsana. *A young boy drags some possessions through the flooded streets of Metro Manila on September 28, 2009.*
Photo credit: ADB.

affected global value-chains, and caused economic losses estimated at $43 billion (Munich Re 2015). In 2012, the year-long drought in the US Midwest caused losses amounting to $30 billion, mostly in harvest failures (Baskin-Gerwitz 2013). The yearly monsoon floods that batter Pakistan and hound millions of people a year have cost the country over $15 billion since 2010 (EM-DAT Database).

Enter Climate Change

The power and fury of Super Typhoon Haiyan that tore through central Philippines in late 2013 and claimed several thousand lives have seen few parallels in recorded history. While the Philippines is not new to typhoons, it was not prepared for the fury of Haiyan.

With sustained winds of 315 kilometers per hour, Haiyan is the strongest typhoon on record ever to make landfall.

It is difficult to pin the intensity of Haiyan on climate change, but the incidence of extreme events and intense climate-related disasters in recent past just as the warming trend is becoming more apparent is both troubling and revealing. The 2015 European heatwave was widespread and led to record highs in Austria, France, Spain, and the United

Kingdom. In the United States, 623 climatic stations set maximum daily record highs in a span of one week (WMO 2015).

In 2011, Thailand confronted a degree of flooding it was unfamiliar with. Records since 1945 show no reports of flooding that proximate the 2011 floods (AON Benfield 2012). While there are several factors associated with the 2011 floods such as urbanization, land subsidence, and insufficient drainage and flood protection systems, the excessive rainfall stands out. The year broke daily and monthly rainfall records, and was the wettest year since 1951. Rains were over 300 percent above normal for March of that year (TMD 2012).

In 2010, the Russian Federation experienced the longest unprecedented heatwave for at least thousand years leaving fifteen thousand people dead. Wild fires enveloped 1,740 square kilometers and destroyed millions of tons of wheat crops. The extremely high surface temperatures associated with the wild fires have a return period of four hundred years (NOAA National Centers for Environmental Information 2010).

The increasing incidence of climate-related disasters refers to floods (hydrological events), storms and temperature extremes (meteorological events), and droughts and wildfires (climatological events), but not to earthquakes and volcanic eruptions (geophysical events).[2] Globally, hydrological disasters have risen fourfold over the past four decades, from an average of forty-five events per year in the decade 1975–1984 to over 180 events per year in the decade 2005–2014. Meteorological disasters more than doubled, from an average of forty-five events a year to almost 120 events a year in comparable periods.[3] Geophysical events, meanwhile, rose from an average of twenty-one events a year to thirty-one events a year over the same four decades.

This observed upsurge in extreme weather-related events underlines the worrisome connection between natural disasters and climate change, driven by significant shifts in average weather conditions or in weather patterns.[4] The ferocity of climate-related disasters, especially hydrometeorological ones, is an emerging threat and one of the central features of the new reality. Hydrometeorological disasters are especially prevalent and destructive in Asia and the Pacific. For this reason, this book has heavy emphasis on hydrometeorological disasters in the region.

New evidence, especially relating to natural disasters, quantifies the economic cost of unabated climate change, with a time frame that is shrinking from the distant future to the next decade or two. These

3

estimates indicate that avoiding such damages would be good for sustaining economic growth. The implication goes further. With losses in physical and human capital and disruptions in productive activities, it is going to be increasingly hard to grow economically in a sustained way unless climate change is confronted.

As global temperatures rise, more and more of these unprecedented disasters take place. Disasters' association with human-induced climate change has changed the perspectives. People are no longer mere victims and human action contributes to the making of disasters.

Climate change adds a new dimension to the age old problem of natural disasters. The link between anthropogenic greenhouse gas (GHG) emissions and global temperatures connects climate change to human actions. Anthropogenic or human-induced climate change alters the character of natural hazards, from that inherent in the physical world, outside the realm of human influence, to phenomena shaped and induced by human activities—particularly the high carbon lifestyle. For lack of a better term, this book uses the term natural disaster to refer to events originating from natural hazards, even as studies and evidence point to human activities influencing these hazards.

Energy-intensive and carbon-intensive human activities have increased GHG emissions and its main component, carbon dioxide (CO_2), in the atmosphere.[5] This in turn has been associated with a rise in long-term average temperatures of the seas and the atmosphere, as well as extreme temperatures and more intense rainfalls—all linked to climate change (IPCC 2012b, 2013).

This association shifts the focus of disasters from purely natural phenomena to human-induced events. This understanding brings to the fore climate change mitigation and adaptation, in addition to the usual disaster preparedness and prevention. All these put the spotlight on how human decisions and actions affect the frequency and severity of climate-related disasters.

Mitigation and Prevention

Reacting to disasters has always been a part of the region's agenda. What is different is the realization of the importance of prevention and preemptive action. It is no longer enough to mop up after a flood; we must turn off the tap. Climate change mitigation is now understood to be within the bounds of human capacity and responsibility. The call to action is spurred by the understanding that the severity of climate-related hazards is induced by human activity. The urgency is prompted by the realization that climate change is a reality today, and that postponing action any further is a recklessness the world cannot afford.

With the rise in the frequency of intense events, climate change mitigation and adaptation, and disaster risk reduction (DRR) and management will need to be scaled up to protect the gains of socioeconomic progress and to prevent it from declining (box 1.1).

Box 1.1. Definitions from the Intergovernmental Panel on Climate Change.

Disaster risk reduction. Policy objectives and measures that anticipate disaster risk, reduce existing exposure, hazard, or vulnerability, and improve resilience.

Disaster risk management. Processes for designing, implementing, and evaluating strategies and policies for disaster risk reduction.

Mitigation of disaster risk. The lessening of the adverse impacts of hazards, including those that are human-induced, through actions that reduce hazard, exposure, and vulnerability.

Mitigation of climate change. Human interventions that reduce the sources of and enhance the sinks of GHGs.

Adaptation. The process of adjustment to actual or expected climate and its effects to moderate harm or exploit beneficial opportunities.

Source: IPCC (2012a).

DRR should not be treated as a cost, but as an investment for saving people's lives, livelihoods, and infrastructures. Mainstreaming disaster resilience and prevention programs will become critical for sustaining growth, especially in economically vibrant cities and regions. In the same way, initiatives toward low-carbon and cleaner options in energy and transport should not be viewed as the whims of green activists but as sensible economic decisions.

When a disaster strikes it is crucial to ensure functioning lifelines, notably safe water access, hospitals and emergency shelters. By making these key installations more disaster-resistant, the impact of disasters is minimized and losses are reduced.

Relief and recovery for the affected should get top priority. To recover with care and to rebuild better in anticipation of future events is likewise essential. Disasters do recur and the world can no longer afford to lag in preparedness and action.

The recently adopted Sendai Framework for Disaster Risk Reduction 2015 reiterates the need to integrate DRR into development measures.

Well-prepared recovery and renovation activities (ahead of disasters) will ensure that capacities are in place for effective response, and make building back better more plausible.

The adage—an ounce of prevention is worth a pound of cure—is evident in a number of examples (Kelman 2013). In the Philippines, with floods preventing children from going to school and crops reaching the market, investing in footbridges at key locations has had high payoffs. In Pakistan, building floodwalls and retention ponds along the Lai River saved money and lives.

Early warning systems and disaster awareness in the school curriculum saved lives in the 2011 Tohoku earthquake in Japan. Keeping drainage facilities functional or conserving forests can go a long way toward reducing a hazard's impact. Garbage-clogged drainage canals were a major factor impeding the runoff of Typhoon Ketsana's rainfall in Manila in 2009. Since then, several local communities with the help of nongovernment organizations and the private sector have cleaned up these canals in highly successful greening programs, such as the one at Estero de Paco.

Natural hazards are inherent in our world, but their severity and impacts can be minimized with disaster mitigation. Unfortunately, disaster prevention is not yet seen as a high priority for stemming the damages from natural disasters. Losses due to natural disasters are still largely considered as costs to be borne after a hazard strikes. While there has been significant progress in the development of early warning systems, there are major gaps especially in low-income countries, where local capacities are highly uneven. Most disaster management agencies rely on emergency funding, making disaster preparedness investments under-resourced. Even where they strike with frequency and regularity, natural disasters are considered as one-off events and not enough is done to diminish their ferocity and impacts.

The Fourth Asian Ministerial Conference on Disaster Risk Reduction in 2010 sought 2 percent of development assistance to finance DRR. In contrast, in the period 1991–2010, DRR was allotted 0.4 percent of total official development assistance. Governments should not be depending on development assistance for DRR. Just as governments try to cushion financial shocks, so too should they invest in cutting disaster risk, as its consequences can be just as grave. Protecting physical and human capital from disasters must be regarded as a government mandate, akin to providing public services. One recommended level of government DRR spending is 1 percent to 2 of national budgets (Darwanto 2012).

Climate mitigation is yet to be seen as a high priority in the context of disaster management. Atmospheric CO_2 concentrations continue to increase and energy subsidies continue to be vast (Coady et al. 2015). Though in varying degrees and quality, all countries need to act on climate change mitigation and DRR, including climate adaptation. The scale of policies needs a sharp shift to match existing knowledge about climate change.

Governments striving for fiscal balance will likely face funding constraints, especially for big-ticket infrastructure projects needed to make cities more resilient. However, the cost of not upping the game in adaptation and disaster preparedness today will result in a slower pace of social and economic progress in affected regions in the decades to come.

The policy implications are twofold. First, DRR needs to be featured in development strategies. Reducing people's exposure and vulnerability through better climate adaptation measures are also essential elements in reducing disaster impacts. Second, climate action, specifically a shift to low-carbon growth, needs to be added as a crucial dimension in disaster prevention.

Weak political will holds back progress in this respect just as much as constraints in technical solutions and inadequate financing. In part, vested interests block environmental steps that are good for the global economy. In addition, there is the ill-informed fear that climate measures are at loggerheads with economic prospects, while the opposite is the case.

The Knowledge–Action Gap

If the climate–disaster link is increasingly evident and the emerging scenario frightening, so too is the disconnect between that knowledge and action. The legacy of inaction to date continues to contribute to rising atmospheric CO_2 concentrations.

Powerful economic forces, in particular, oil and fossil-fuel-dependent energy companies, have a clear interest in keeping the world economy on a high-carbon path. However, there are three other factors that deserve serious attention in explaining this knowledge–action gap.

First, uncertainties on the exact time when a hazard will occur increases society's inactivity on actions. It is also often assumed that the severe effects of climate change will not be felt in our lifetimes. Under various scenarios, the sea level rise for 2081–2100 is projected to be in the range of 0.26 meters to 0.82 meters, due to increased ocean warming and loss of mass from glaciers and ice sheets (IPCC 2013). Since 2100 seems very far into the future, and less than a meter increase seems too small, people get a false sense of complacency. But it is likely that the increase in storm surges since 1970s is already a result of rising sea levels (IPCC 2014c).

Second, climate action is seen to be a global responsibility, which can also mean that it is nobody's responsibility. It does not help that the gains and consequences from individual action are seen to accrue, at least in part, to others. This is a paramount example of the tragedy of the commons, whereby individual actions for individual gain, though seemingly harmless, add up to be detrimental for all. Like the problems of over-grazing and over-fishing which leave pastures and seas degraded and no longer fit to sustain cattle and fish, everybody can turn a blind eye to the deteriorating natural environment as they continue to reap the gains of high-carbon activities. Local politics everywhere has eschewed measures whose perceived benefits are partly global and only partly local.

While international agreements have remained elusive the past decades, people are very hopeful with the adoption of the climate agreement forged at the 21st Conference of the Parties (COP21) of the United Nations Framework Convention on Climate Change in Paris in December 2015. Responding to the initial submission of post 2020 mitigation targets of individual countries, executive secretary of the UNFCCC Christiana Figueres is confident, "the breadth and depth of this response reflects the increasing recognition that there is an unparalleled opportunity to achieve resilient, low-emission, sustainable development at the national level" (UNFCCC Newsroom 2015). This COP21 agreement among 195 countries calls for a shift away from fossil fuels and encourages vast amounts of capital to be spent on climate mitigation and adaptation. The agreement also contains a provision requiring developed countries to collectively raise $100 billion annually by 2020, to finance developing countries' climate efforts. And while the impact of the collective submissions still fall short of the estimated required reductions to limit warming to 2°C, these signal an important move away from business-as-usual fossil dependence.

Countries can take unilateral action without waiting for multilateral accords, especially when local and global gains overlap. Indeed, many countries did just that for trade liberalization. Climate reform could follow a similar track.

In November 2014, the People's Republic of China and the United States made a joint agreement on climate change and clean energy. The People's Republic of China will increase the non-fossil-fuel share of all energy to 20 percent and peak emissions by 2030. The United States will cut net GHG emissions by 26 percent–28 percent below 2005 levels by 2025. Based on the 2015 study of the London School of Economics and Grantham Research Institute of ninety-nine countries, climate action is beginning to show a very positive trend. There are now seventy-five countries plus the European Union which have national laws and policies to address climate mitigation; forty-five of these have economy-wide emission targets.

High-carbon growth leads to environmental degradation which affects local communities the most. Beijing's residents are suffering the health impacts of high pollution levels mostly attributed to the use of coal for energy and more vehicles on the road. Pollution in India is also estimated to shorten the life expectancies of some six hundred million of its population by some three years (Greenstone et al. 2015). India is home to thirteen of the twenty most polluted cities in the world (WHO 2014a). In the United States, the Obama administration's dramatic proposal to slash carbon emissions from power plants to 30 percent below the 2005 level by 2030 offers health gains as well as the potential to spur global action. Cutting back on black carbon emissions will make local populations breathe better and have a salutary impact on climate change. With rising concerns over the typhoon and monsoon seasons in Asia, and the Atlantic hurricane season in North America, the payoffs are tangible.

Third, responding to climate change is believed to cut into economic growth. Many see climate investments as incompatible with economic growth. From this viewpoint, switching to a low-carbon path is seen as costly and hence conflicts with economic growth.

One aspect of this resistance is the absence of climate change and its implications in the economic calculus of decisions. While scientists project the economic impacts of runaway climate change, economists are for the most part projecting economic growth rates unaffected by climate scenarios. While the global economic impact of climate change is very difficult to assess, climate change impacts are projected to erode food security, increase displacement of people, create new poverty pockets, and slow economic growth.

The United Nations intergovernmental forum tasked to formulate the Sustainable Development Goals acknowledges this knowledge-action gap and intends to reduce this through the development of a science-policy interface. Given the complexity of climate science, strengthening the science and policy-making link will help form appropriate frameworks for action and will highly enrich the decision-making process.

Pursuit of Economic Growth

The relationship between growth and natural capital is real, and economics literature and policy advice have to reflect that reality. Mainstream economic advice, by and large, has seen environmental protection as a cost to growth rather than a path to sustainable growth. At the root of this misplaced guidance are growth models which are at best silent on the cost of environmental damage for economic growth, and at worst see environmental destruction as a necessary accompaniment of growth. This will have to change.

Economies will have to take a green growth path—despite having been accustomed to the unsustainable practices of extraction and pollution, and dependence on fossil fuels. In doing this, countries will be forced to rely less on the indiscriminate exploitation of natural capital and natural assets and be mindful of the alarming rise in global warming.

Stiglitz (2013) suggested that given the global economic slowdown, retrofitting of the global economy for climate change would be a source of aggregate demand and economic growth.

While the pressure to shift sides will come most visibly from within, as natural disasters become regular manifestations of the changing climate, pressure to change will also come externally, as competitive forces unleash new technological changes and usher resilient economies based on sustainable development elsewhere. Compulsion to cross over to the green side will be heightened by rivalry among nations, as being environmentally sustainable may soon become a new determinant of economic and social as well as political strength.

Adopting green growth policies and a green accounting approach which incorporates the valuation of ecosystem services in national income accounts will reflect the relative scarcity of natural capital and the sometimes irreversibility of ecological damage. This will help reduce extensive profiteering from extractive industries by bringing to light the true costs of these activities. The green accounting approach also provides a better measure of trade-offs than mainstream national income accounting.

Several steps can be taken that are simultaneously good for economic growth and a low-carbon and sustainable environment. These win-win options include eliminating fossil-fuel subsidies, although even here special interests are likely to oppose subsidy reform. Green investments will also bring about socioeconomic gains, and here climate action will be a necessary investment. Growth and the reduction of climate risks, with the right mix of policies, technology, and investments, can be mutually reinforcing.

Policies to protect mangrove forests is another win-win example. Mangrove forests protect coastal areas against storms and sea surges. Mangrove protection is also good for community livelihoods by maintaining breeding grounds for fisheries and sources of wood, fostering growth. The proposed Sustainable Development Goals focus on the deterioration of coastal and marine resources, suggesting severe and immediate negative impacts for the most vulnerable if these ecosystems continue to be degraded. In the meantime, policies that encourage deforestation and the destruction of other natural capital are commonplace. Producer and consumer subsidies worldwide continue to encourage energy intensity, emissions, and waste.

It would therefore be prudent to strategically manage nonrenewable resources and green fuels today to prepare for a cleaner growth path. If not, the costs of retooling carbon-intensive infrastructure would become exorbitantly high later and exceedingly difficult to manage.

The economic effects of natural disasters are also assumed to have discontinuous, short-lived, or nominal impacts, and they are viewed as blips or temporary drags on the inexorable path of economic progress. Some offer the idea that the impact of climate change on the global economy is likely to be quite small over the next fifty years, that climate change's impact through tropical storms would be minor, and that coastal protection would check sea level rise (Mendelsohn 2009; Tol 2011). Some literature on the economics of climate change use arbitrary inputs and assume modest costs and impacts without an empirical or theoretical basis. These writings underestimate climate change impacts and neglect the possibility of catastrophic climate outcomes (Stern 2013b, Pindyck 2013).

Impacts on long-term growth are generally rejected. By this thinking, disasters are not seen to hurt growth, nor does investment in disaster prevention help to sustain a better growth rate than otherwise. Rehabilitation and reconstruction, meanwhile, is associated with small and positive impacts on growth to the extent that there is increased spending.

Some say that loss and destruction during intense disasters can boost long-term economic growth by providing countries an opening to renew old capital stocks and embrace better technologies improving total factor productivity (Skidmore and Toya 2002). These results used disaster frequency data alone and may have failed to measure the actual level of disaster risks by excluding damage and casualty costs in the disaster-growth equation (Kim 2010). Natural disasters viewed this way are unlikely to be a source for creating net growth and measures to lessen impact and reduce future losses will actually minimize disruptions to growth.

A reverse analogy may suggest ways to address these issues. Imagine that climate change hurt those who contribute most to GHG emissions. Imagine also that climate impacts are immediate. Climate action in this scenario would be strong and happening now. Such a scenario will enable us to break out of the growth versus environment dilemma. Steps would follow to make renewable energy much more affordable. More generally, the price of inaction would be internalized and reflected within the path of economic growth.

Urgent action is needed on two fronts: first, to reduce GHG emissions and second, to help countries prepare for a world of climate and weather extremes. Acting on natural disasters and disaster prevention issues could be in a country's own benefit, especially from the perspective of growth. Indeed, disaster risk management can be a profitable investment. Even simple preparedness measures against natural hazards and disasters can catalyze a green growth process. Think of long stretches of green walls along vulnerable coastlines or the green jobs that would be created by rebuilding vast expanses of forests and mangroves.

DRR and adaptation can help improve and protect agricultural productivity and therefore growth. In urban settings, this can go hand in hand with resilience building, inducing growth through stronger and better-adapted city plans and infrastructure.

Investing in the capacity for disaster preparedness and prevention can help improve the profitability of business investments which generates growth. New York's disaster preparedness and prevention efforts after Hurricane Sandy helped boost confidence among investors and businesses, leverage private investments, and induce growth.

Indeed it may be imprudent to wait for disasters to unfold rather than use DRR as a game-changer for development plans and policies. A great deal of global manufacturing and other economic activities are in exceptionally hazard-prone and ill-prepared areas. Natural disasters are also taking a heavier toll on more densely populated, poorer, and more environmentally degraded areas. Another alarming trend is the increasing mortality and economic losses of smaller-scale and recurrent local disasters.

Disaster prevention can complement the traditional growth efforts by involving businesses and the research community to foster innovations and to make the disaster insurance market viable and profitable. The relationship between disasters and growth is also strengthened because prevention measures are seen to mimic technological improvements in the reconstruction process.

Meanwhile, the growth implications of working with new disaster insurance companies and risk markets are gaining traction. It is beginning to be recognized that the management of endemic disaster risks lead to the development of disaster insurance markets, which could have a strong potential to catalyze other industry-wide investments or spur new economic activities as in most developed countries.

Since natural disasters are not treated as systemic risks, disaster planning and risk management are not seized as opportunities for stimulating growth. Prevention projects continue to be ranked low on the priority list. And when they are taken into account, they are often simply made a small part of a large infrastructure project.

With the cost of efforts and trade-offs involved, efficiency is needed in the transition to a green economy. It also calls for the development of markets for disaster prevention, services, and technologies, and a greater role for the private sector to get involved. Multilateral development banks can help leverage private sector interests for environmental goals.

A switch to a disaster resilient, green economy has yet to take place. It is difficult to undo the carbon-based edifice of modern civilization that has contributed to extreme hazards and intense natural disasters. Reconciling growth with greenness requires an increase in abatement paths, market-based incentives, and carbon efficiency. It also calls for de-carbonizing energy sources and developing new low-carbon technologies, and enlarging carbon sinks, among others.

Climate response is in an economy's own growth interest. A shift to a low-carbon path now will lower future climate and disaster losses, lower future mitigation costs, and pave the way for a more sustainable growth.

Climate Crisis and Response

The urgency to act is heightened by the observed effects of a warming world: shrinking glaciers, decreasing crop yields, and irreversible sea level rise from ice sheet loss.

Immediate action is also compounded by the knowledge that delaying mitigation increases mitigation costs.

Delaying emission reduction measures means continuing accumulation and higher CO_2 concentrations. Higher CO_2 concentrations and higher temperatures are associated with disproportionately higher damages. Once global warming reaches a tipping point, climate change then becomes a self-amplifying cycle (Furman, Shadbegian, and Stock 2015).

Steps to protect coastlines and low-lying urban areas from rising sea levels and flooding, and prevent farm yields from declining due to changing climatic trends, are key to containing climate costs. With cities at the core of economic activities, more must be done to protect them from storms and floods. Since 2011, extreme weather events or climate change have consistently ranked within the top five global risks in terms of likelihood and impact—and yet very little progress has been made in terms of climate action and disaster prevention (WEF 2015). Despite the evidence of the economic damage from climate change, few politicians have successfully run for national office vowing to confront the problem.

This raises a troubling conundrum. Without a political mandate, climate mitigation will continue to lag; and without action, runaway climate change will hurt lives and livelihoods and impede economic growth. It is therefore vital to seize every opportunity to turn perceptions around, exploit windows of opportunity, and build on win-win options.

The fall in oil prices which began in the second half of 2014 presents a rare opportunity to let go of these subsidies without the economic and political repercussions of high oil prices—as India and Indonesia have already demonstrated.

The ongoing global negotiations on climate targets and commitments present another opportunity. In comparison to their history of failure, these negotiations have shown signs of life, with, as noted earlier, the United States and the People's Republic of China committing, even if not in a binding way, to meaningful targets. The new agreement adopted at the COP21 Paris climate conference in December 2015, to be implemented beginning 2020, presents a fresh opening.

The crucial question is whether the emerging climate crisis will trigger national and worldwide environmental actions in time. This will happen if we realize that the risks are both local and global, that they affect the present and the future, and that it is climate inaction, not action, that will derail economic growth.

Notes

1. The term natural disasters differentiates this set of disasters from events originating from industrial, transport, and other technological accidents. In this book, the term natural disasters includes geophysical, climatological, hydrological, and meteorological, and does not include biological disasters (epidemics, insect infestations, animal stampedes) and extraterrestrial disasters.

2. See Appendix Table 1 for the detailed classification of natural disasters used by the Emergency Events Database (EM-DAT).

3. Disaster statistics are based on EM-DAT, a longitudinal dataset on the occurrence and impacts of natural disasters worldwide compiled by the Center for Research on Epidemiology of Disasters (CRED). It is based on reported events causing at least ten deaths, affecting at least hundred people, or prompting a declaration of a state of emergency or a call for international assistance.

4. The Intergovernmental Panel on Climate Change defines climate change as "a change in the state of the climate that can be identified (e.g., by using statistical tests) by changes in the mean and/or the variability of its properties, and that persists for an extended period, typically decades or longer." The United Nations Framework Convention on Climate Change defines climate change as "a change of climate which is attributed directly or indirectly to human activity that alters the composition of the global atmosphere and which is in addition to natural climate variability observed over comparable time periods." (IPCC 2014a).

5. Greenhouse gases refer to CO_2, methane (CH_4), nitrous oxide (N_2O), and halocarbons. CO_2 emissions contributed 78 percent of total GHG emissions increase from 1970 to 2010 (IPCC 2014c).

2

The Anatomy of Climate-Related Natural Disasters

*Saving our planet, lifting people out of poverty, advancing economic
growth . . . these are one and the same fight. We must connect the
dots between climate change, water scarcity, energy shortages,
global health, food security and women's empowerment.
Solutions to one problem must be solutions for all.*
—Ban Ki-moon, Secretary-General of the United Nations

The most visible sign of things going off track is the rising incidence
of disasters with a likely link to climate change. Deadly climate-related
disasters have caught the world's attention over the past decade. Con-
current to this is the increased awareness to the backdrop of rising
temperatures, rising sea levels, and shrinking sea ice and glaciers.

Climate science demonstrates how GHG emissions alter atmospheric
GHG concentrations and affect temperature and precipitation, and help
generate climate extremes and hazards. Aside from climate-related
factors, disaster risks also increase as more people are exposed, and
remain weak and defenseless.

Climate-related disaster risk is the expected value of losses often
represented as the probability of occurrence of hazardous events mul-
tiplied by the impacts (effects on lives, livelihoods, health, ecosystems,
economies, societies, cultures, services, and infrastructure) if these
events occur. Risks result from the interaction of three elements:

- **Hazard**. The occurrence of the physical event that may cause loss
  of life, injury, or other health impacts, as well as damage and loss to
  property, infrastructure, livelihoods, service provision, ecosystems,
  and environmental resources.

- **Exposure**. The presence of people, livelihoods, species or ecosystems, environmental functions, services, and resources, infrastructure, or economic, social, or cultural assets in places and settings that could be adversely affected.
- **Vulnerability**. The propensity to be adversely affected, including sensitivity to harm and lack of capacity to cope and adapt.

The framework of climate-related risks as shown in figure 2.1, reveals the various entry points, approaches, and considerations in managing climate-related risks. For instance, land-use policy and climate-sensitive urban design can reduce people's exposure to hazards, thereby reducing risk. In the same manner, communities armed with disaster awareness and preparedness, and supported by adaptive infrastructure can bolster defenses and lessen vulnerability. With respect to hazards, collective decisions and actions to reduce GHG emissions can also slow anthropogenic climate change and reduce its exacerbating effects on hazards.

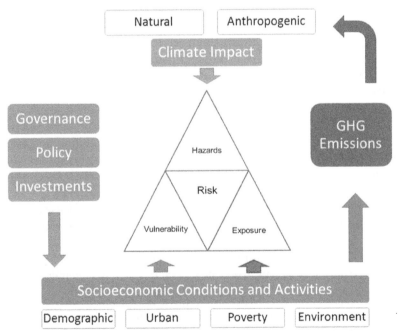

Figure 2.1. Climate-related risk.

Source: Author's illustration adapted from IPCC (2014a).

It would not be accurate to call the deaths wrought by Cyclone Nargis in Myanmar in 2008, or the devastation brought about by floods that submerged Bangkok in 2011 as "natural" disasters, as these calamities are not solely caused by the randomness of nature. There is much that people and the global community can do to reduce risks on the three fronts of hazards, exposure, and vulnerability.

Anthropogenic Link to Climate-Related Hazards

The Intergovernmental Panel on Climate Change (2014c) confirms the Earth's warming atmosphere and oceans, diminishing snow and ice, and rising sea levels, among other changes. GHG concentrations in the atmosphere continue to rise. Land and ocean surface temperature data show an increase of 0.85°C over 1880–2012 temperatures. The three decades starting from 1983 were likely the warmest period in the last fourteen hundred years in the Northern Hemisphere. Greenland and Antarctic ice sheets have been losing mass and glaciers are shrinking worldwide (IPCC 2013). This has spurred scientific studies and debates on if and how human-induced GHG emissions trigger climate change, and if and how climate change exacerbates hazards.

A warming of 2°C above preindustrial levels may be reached in twenty to thirty years (World Bank 2013a). This would cause food shortages in sub-Saharan Africa to become more common. In South Asia, it would induce shifting rain patterns that would leave some areas under water, while others without enough water for power generation, irrigation, or drinking. In Southeast Asia, the degradation and loss of reefs would diminish tourism, reduce fish stocks, and leave coastal communities and cities more vulnerable to increasingly violent storms and landslides. If warming goes to 4°C, multiple threats of more extreme heatwaves, rising sea levels, and more severe storms, droughts, and floods will have dire implications for the poorest and most vulnerable. Without climate-smart development and safety nets in place, climate change can push a hundred million people into extreme poverty by 2030 (Hallegatte et al. 2016).

Since Fourier in 1824 and Tyndall in 1864, scientists have been studying the extent to which human-induced GHG emissions are causing changes in the climate. While some argue that the effects of the dynamic interplay of all the underlying climate change variables are bafflingly difficult to model and predict, the evidence shows that the rise in global average surface temperature from 1951 to 2010

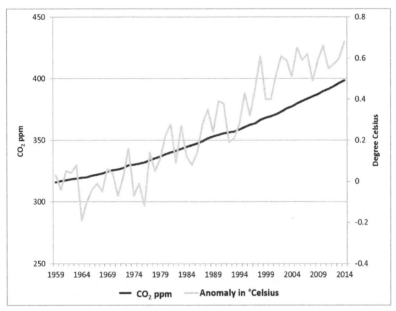

Figure 2.2. Carbon dioxide atmospheric concentrations at Mauna Loa and global annual temperature anomaly: 1959–2014.

ppm = parts per million.
Notes: The CO_2 data measured in ppm on Mauna Loa constitute the longest record of direct measurements of CO_2 in the atmosphere. Global annual mean surface air temperature change, in degree Celsius, base period 1951–1980.
Source: NASA GISS (2015), Tans (2015), Keeling (2015).

was caused by the anthropogenic increase in GHG concentrations (IPCC 2013).

Humans are emitting GHGs into the Earth's atmosphere at a substantial and increasing rate—currently over thirty billion tons of CO_2 a year, along with other GHGs such as methane (CH_4) and nitrous oxide (NO_2). As a result, GHG concentrations in the atmosphere have been rising consistently, as have global surface temperatures (figure 2.2). Increased concentrations of GHGs in the atmosphere are expected to trap more heat on Earth and lead to a gradual increase in global average temperatures.

The warming trend is apparent. The ten hottest years on record since 1880 all occurred after 1997, topped by 2014 (table 2.1). For the 38th consecutive year, average annual temperatures are above the long-term average, and 2015 eclipsed 2014 as the hottest year on record (NOAA National Centers for Environmental Information 2015).

Table 2.1. Ten warmest years on record, 1880–2014.

Rank: 1 = Warmest	Year	Anomaly °C
1	2014	0.69
2 (tie)	2010	0.65
2 (tie)	2005	0.65
4	1998	0.63
5 (tie)	2013	0.62
5 (tie)	2003	0.62
7	2002	0.61
8	2006	0.60
9 (tie)	2009	0.59
9 (tie)	2007	0.59

Source: NOAA NCDC (2015).

Atmospheric CO_2 concentrations surpassed four hundred parts per million (ppm) for three successive months in 2014. The first five months of 2015 averaged 401 ppm CO_2. If CO_2 concentrations continue to increase at a little over 2 ppm annually, as they did during 2005–2014, the planet would be over the 450 ppm mark in a quarter of a century. Scientists consider 450 ppm to be the threshold level above which it will be difficult, if not unlikely, to limit temperature increase to 2°C relative to 1850–1900 levels.

The Amazon is pivotal to the Earth's global carbon cycle, being the largest tropical forest in the world. Higher temperatures will dry vegetation and will likely lead to droughts. (The 2005 and 2010 Amazon droughts coincided with higher than normal tropical North Atlantic sea surface temperatures.) These in turn will lead to increased tree mortality and forest fires, releasing more carbon and further warming the Earth (UNEP GEAS 2011).

Permafrost thawing will also release trapped carbon into the atmosphere, causing more warming, causing more thawing—creating a feedback loop. A large fraction of anthropogenic climate change resulting from CO_2 emissions and ice sheet mass loss are irreversible on a multi-century to millennial time scale (IPCC 2013).

Several studies have identified and have sought to separate the different sources of global mean surface temperature variability (figure 2.3). Their detection and attribution analysis attributed most of the warming over the past fifty years to anthropogenic influence. The contribution of solar variability was minimal and could not have explained the rising temperatures. Internal variability brought about by the Atlantic Multidecadal Oscillation and the El Niño-Southern Oscillation were found to be too small to contribute to the relatively large observed warming since 1950. However, scientists are not totally removing the naturally occurring El Niño in the climate change picture. El Niño and record-high global temperatures may "interact and modify each other in ways which we have never before experienced," according to World Meteorological Organization Secretary-General Michel Jarraud (World Meteorological Organization [WMO] 2015).

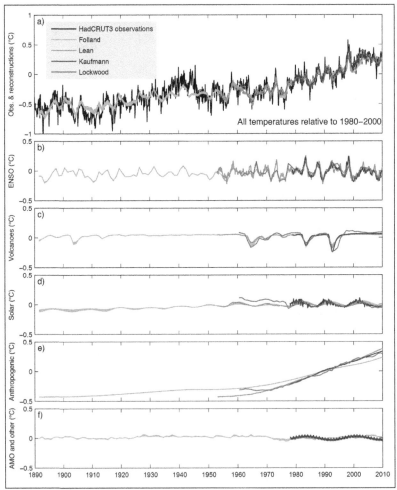

Figure 2.3. Contributions to global mean temperature change, 1890–2010.

Notes: AMO = Atlantic Multidecadal Oscillation; ENSO= El Niño-Southern Oscillation
Source: IPCC (2013).

That human activities result in GHG emissions, and that GHG emissions are the dominant cause of the observed warming of the planet, are scientifically indisputable. The IPCC, in its fifth and latest Assessment Report asserted the anthropogenic link to climate.[1] Based on the more than ten thousand published research on climate from 1991 to 2011, 97 percent of studies expressing a position on anthropogenic global warming endorse it (Cook et al. 2013). In another study of 928 abstracts in refereed journals from 1993 to 2003, none of the evaluated papers disagreed with human-induced climate change (Oreskes 2004). Detailed studies of the 2003 European heatwave and the winter time droughts in the Mediterranean region confirm that human-induced climate change played a role in magnifying the likelihood of occurrences of these hazards (Stott, Stone, and Allen 2004; Hoerling et al. 2012).

Human-induced climate change has also been linked to the increase in heatwaves (Coumou and Rahmstorf 2012). There is evidence to conclude with 80 percent probability that the 2010 Moscow heatwaves that killed eleven thousand people would not have occurred without human-induced climate warming (Rahmstorf and Coumou 2011). The record high temperature of 2014 which was driven by human activities exacerbated the California 2012–2014 drought by 36 percent, making it the worst recorded drought in the past twelve hundred years (Nuccitelli 2014).[2]

Evidence of anthropogenic GHG emissions contributing to the observed intensification of precipitation events were found in two-thirds of the Northern Hemisphere regions (Min et al. 2011). Atmospheric thermodynamics explain that the moisture-holding capacity of the atmosphere is largely influenced by temperature and pressure, and that warmer atmospheres have larger saturation vapor content. The median intensity of extreme precipitation increases with near-surface temperature at a rate of 5.9 –7.7 percent per degree (Westra, Alexander, and Zwiers 2013). This could even reach as high as 14 percent per degree when daily mean temperatures exceed 12°C. Even short duration precipitation extremes can cause local flooding, erosion, and water damage.

Climate change models indicate that the risk of floods occurring in England and Wales in autumn 2000 was significantly higher by at least 20 percent due to twentieth-century anthropogenic GHG emissions (Pall et al. 2011). Case studies on three catchment regions in southeastern Australia show that doubling CO_2 scenarios will increase the frequency and magnitude of flood events with significant building damages (Schreider, Smith, and Jakeman 2000). Records from Japan's automated meteorological stations situated all over the country show that precipitation events exceeding 50 mm and 80 mm per hour have increased from the 1970s to 2013 (JMA 2014).

Tropical cyclones are areas of low atmospheric pressure over tropical and subtropical waters with huge, circulating mass of winds, with speeds of at least 119 kilometers per hour, and thunderstorms with spans of hundreds of kilometers. Aside from destructive winds, tropical cyclones can bring torrential rain, storm surges, and tornadoes that can ruin population centers, agricultural land, and metropolises.[3]

For cyclones to form, warm ocean waters of at least 26.5°C throughout a depth of at least 50 meters are necessary to form the warm moist air they need. Below this temperature, the atmosphere is too stable and thunderstorms are not created. As warm air rises into the atmosphere, air cools and condenses into water droplets or clouds. As water vapor condenses, heat is released. If upper level winds are weak, this heat provides the energy to drive tropical cyclone formation. This heat further warms the atmosphere causing air to rise further. This frees space for more air to move in, causing the strong winds of storms. This basic physiology of cyclones explains how unusually warm waters brought about by global warming and climate change can lead to more intense cyclone events.

Global warming is also projected to increase sea levels. As sea levels rise, the potential for storm surges to move further inland increases. A coastal storm surge drives large volumes of water ashore at high speed and immense force. In 1970, Cyclone Bhola's massive storm surge left some three hundred thousand to five hundred thoudand people dead in the coastal wetlands of Bangladesh.

Studies predict that doubling atmospheric CO_2 concentrations will triple the number of Category 5 storms (Anderson and Bausch 2006). Studies also predict that for every 1°C rise in global temperature the frequency of events of the magnitude of Hurricane Katrina will increase by at least two times, and possibly as much as seven times (Grinsted, Moore, and Jevrejeva 2013).[4] Climate models project a 3 percent–5 percent increase in wind speed per degree Celsius increase of tropical sea surface temperatures (WMO 2006), while some projections indicate that the intensity of tropical cyclones will increase by 2 percent–11 percent by 2100 (Knutson et al. 2010). With climate change, global losses from hurricanes may double (Hallegatte 2012).

Since the 1970s, the potential destructiveness of hurricanes has increased considerably and this has been shown to be highly correlated with tropical sea surface temperature. With storm lifetimes and intensities increasing by at least 50 percent, the destructive potential of a cyclone, as measured by its power dissipation,[5] has more than doubled in the Atlantic and increased by 75 percent in the Pacific (Emanuel 2005).

The rise in sea surface temperatures is the "main determinant of the strength of storms, the total column water vapor and the convective available potential energy" (Trenberth, 2005). Hurricane Sandy—the deadliest and most destructive hurricane of the 2012 Atlantic hurricane season—was fueled by unusually warm ocean waters. Sandy produced storm surges almost 6 meters high, resulting in massive flooding that shut down the Port of New York and New Jersey for five days.

From 1975 to 2004, global hurricane data reveals that Category 4 and 5 hurricanes have almost doubled in number, from fifty every five years in the 1970s to almost ninety every five years in the 2000s (Webster et al. 2005). The weakest storms (Category 1) decreased in number over this period.

Typhoon Haiyan formed when the sea surface temperature of the Pacific Warm Pool Region was at its highest (based on records since 1981) and the sea surface temperature of the West Pacific Region was elevated (Comiso, Perez, and Stock 2015). The continuing increase of these temperatures must be taken as a portent of things to come, given the correlation between sea surface temperatures and maximum winds of typhoons.

The El Niño-Southern Oscillation will remain the dominant mode of yearly variability in the tropical Pacific with global effects. At the same time there is an emerging consensus that the overall frequency of various extreme events will continue to rise due to anthropogenic global warming. The convergence of anthropogenic factors and natural variability in extreme events could be catastrophic. For instance, the increase in moisture availability is likely to intensify El Niño-related precipitation variability on regional scales.

Exposure

Exposure is the presence of people, livelihoods, ecosystems, environmental services, resources, infrastructure, and economic, social, and cultural assets in places and settings that could be adversely affected by natural hazards.

The roughly eighty tropical storms that form every year are from seven cyclone basins: Atlantic, North Indian, Southeast Indian, Southwest Indian, Northeast Pacific, Northwest Pacific, and Southwest Pacific. People living along cyclone tracks and near the coasts of these basins expect these yearly events. Similarly, people living in low-lying coastal areas and floodplains susceptible to monsoon flooding are used to heavy seasonal rains. But more people and industries are now settling in such hazard-prone areas, putting themselves in harm's way.

Clearly, a climate-related hazard might not create a disaster if it strikes where there are no communities or economic activity. An intense storm in a sparsely populated area will pose less risk than a moderate storm in a densely populated city.

Increasing economic damages from tropical cyclones in recent years may be explained by the increasing wealth in locations prone to these cyclones. Some suggest that the value of tropical cyclone losses and damage may double just because of increasing incomes (Mendelsohn et al. 2012).

Data from the reinsurance industry suggest that societal change in population and wealth is sufficient to explain increasing disaster losses (Mohleji and Pielke 2014). An analysis of twenty-two disaster loss studies suggests that disaster loss trends can be attributed to increases in population and capital (Bouwer 2011). Some argue that this may be especially true for rising urban centers with their increasing populations and the buildup of assets and infrastructure.

Clearly, exposure is a big factor in disasters. Strong economic considerations drive exposure. Communities and industries are built in flood-prone coastal areas because of the economic opportunities and services these areas provide, such as harbors and ports, livelihoods,

Figure 2.4. Typhoon Haiyan devastates coastal cities. *Communities were flattened by container vans swept ashore from a nearby port.*

Photo credit: ADB.

and transportation (figure 2.4). The infrastructure and market access of these areas offer comparative advantages which become more persuasive as economies become more global.

With these inherent advantages, coastal areas have higher productivity than inland areas. In the People's Republic of China, total factor productivity in coastal provinces is 85 percent higher than inland provinces. The bearing of geography and transportation is further demonstrated by the disadvantages of landlocked countries which have, on average, slower growth than coastal countries. And then again, the number of megacities in regions at risk of flooding, particularly Dhaka, Kolkata, Manila, Mumbai, and Shanghai, suggest an economic judgment that despite the inherent risks, people choose to establish lives and businesses in these areas.

With these cities becoming national and regional growth centers, the rationale of choosing these high-risk regions is demonstrated. Once the impetus is established, agglomeration economies set in, further increasing investments, in-migration, and population density. The continuing rise in human and economic exposure in high-risk megacities cannot be discounted. By 2030, Shanghai's current population of twenty-three million is expected to balloon to thirty-one million, and Dhaka is estimated to add another ten million to its present seventeen million population (UN DESA 2014). Understanding the economic decisions that led to the situation of having more people living in harm's way is necessary for managing the exposure dimensions of risks.

Appreciating the enormity of risks is vital for policy reforms and change of mindset to reduce exposure. Investments that take into consideration the advantages of location and agglomeration economies, and ignore disaster risk, are clearly not sustainable. Economic calculations that put more weight on short-term profits and excessively mark down future risks must be reviewed.

Reducing disaster risk cannot be dealt with in isolation from economic and social considerations. For instance, a simple zoning law that prohibits houses to be built near the coast will not succeed if people's livelihoods are based along the coast (fishing, tourism, ports), especially if there are no alternative livelihoods and no accessible transportation services. A more holistic approach would consider building new communities with livelihood opportunities or investing in new roads and transport services, allowing people to live in safe areas but work in vulnerable areas. These strategies and activities should be part of development plans.

Measures that can identify citizens who are more likely to take on more risks in exchange for income opportunities must be established, together with policies to steer and support them toward risk-reducing behavior and decisions. For instance, at very low levels of income people may choose to take on additional risks for the opportunity to earn more. Marginalized sectors opt to live under city bridges, along river banks, and along railroad tracks for the accompanying income opportunities of these locations. As people become better off, they tend to prefer the safer and less risk prone areas and structures. Some suggest that disaster impact as a function of wealth is not necessarily monotonically increasing or decreasing (Kellenberg and Mobarak 2008). There is an inverted-U relationship; that is, disaster losses increase with income before they decrease.

Vulnerability

Not all people and assets will be affected by hazards such as flooding and cyclones in the same way. Differences in physical, behavioral, and economic characteristics influence the propensity of people and assets to be harmed, and the lack of capacity to cope and adapt. A multidimensional concept, vulnerability to climate change is a function of non-climatic determinants such as wealth and other demographic and socioeconomic factors.

There are opposing forces on people's vulnerability. Environmental degradation has rendered many locations increasingly vulnerable to floods and storms. On the other hand, there has been progress in disaster risk management. With more accurate forecasting, improved early warning systems, and better evacuation procedures in place, fatalities from such events have fallen, even as their occurrence and level of damages have risen.

Vulnerability, like exposure, is also influenced by socioeconomic factors. Several studies find that income, education, and institutions shape vulnerabilities and, subsequently, natural disaster impacts (Brooks, Adger, and Kelly 2005; Kahn 2005; Noy 2008; Rentschler 2013; Kellenberg and Mobarak 2008). Thomas, Albert, and Hepburn (2014) examined the importance of climate hazards (measured by climate anomalies) as a determinant of disaster risk in Asia and the Pacific, along with population exposure and vulnerability. Exposure and vulnerability can either act independently or simultaneously, often creating synergies or even creating a cycle of increasing or decreasing risk.

Natural hazards are income blind, affecting both developed and developing countries. Poorer economies are hit harder. Studies have shown how fatality rates and economic losses as a proportion of GDP are higher in developing countries. The higher share of impoverished populations in vulnerable urban zones with weak infrastructure makes for stronger impact in developing countries. Weak government capacity and lack of basic facilities also increase susceptibility to disasters.

Cyclone Nargis and Hurricane Sandy are indications that both developing and developed countries face climate-related disaster risks. Deaths, injuries, displacements, damages, and disaster impact in both groups of countries are affected by hazard intensity, exposure, and vulnerability. Awareness, preparedness, technological progress, and DRR have clearly reduced deaths from comparable hazards. The numbers of people affected have nevertheless been on the rise everywhere. Economic damages from comparable events are greater in developed countries, indicative of higher-valued assets and structures, and the higher cost of rebuilding. Deaths from natural disasters concentrate in poorer developing countries.

Poverty reduction measures and safety nets are part of disaster mitigation and resilience building. Flash floods commonly cause more fatalities in poorer communities than in more affluent areas. Poorer segments of the population with scant resources often end up in the higher-risk peripheral areas, and often also have little protection in poorly built homes. When disaster strikes, they are often left with even less resources. And when livelihoods are affected, losses are further amplified, leaving people even more vulnerable.

Typhoon Haiyan, for example, struck Eastern Visayas, one of the poorest regions of the Philippines, where four out of every ten families are poor (PSA 2013). While damages from natural disasters in that year cost the country roughly 0.9 percent of its national product, Haiyan-related losses in the Eastern Visayas amounted to 17.4 percent of its regional product (NEDA 2013). With very little coping capacity, many Haiyan victims were still living in tents some eighteen months after the disaster, and some twenty thousand remain displaced as of 2015 (IDMC 2015).

When disasters hit lower-middle and low-income countries, they are usually overwhelmed by the huge rebuilding costs. While absolute average annual losses of high-income countries from disasters are much higher compared to lower-income countries, these losses would hardly make a dent in rich countries' economies and social development. Low-income countries would end up incurring average annual losses equivalent to 22 percent of social spending. The comparable figure for rich countries would be less than 2 percent (UNISDR 2015a).

Evidence shows that higher educational attainment and literacy are associated with better disaster management and adaptive capacity (Brooks, Adger, and Kelly 2005; Toya and Skidmore 2007).

In the case of the 2004 Indian Ocean tsunami, there were more female deaths than males. Across age groups, children below ten years and adults above forty years are found to be most vulnerable (Birkmann, Fernando, and Hettige 2007).

Adaptive capacity is associated with governance, and civil and political rights. Countries with strong institutions (such as a strong financial sector), openness to trade, and higher levels of government spending were found to be better able to withstand initial disaster shocks (Kahn 2005; Noy 2008; Toya and Skidmore 2007).

It is vital that institutional and adaptive capacity is strengthened in cities where these are weak, especially in the cities that are highly susceptible to flooding, storm surges, and tropical cyclones. Dhaka is a case in point. Indeed the city is regarded at extreme risk from climate change.

Notes

1. IPCC assessments are written by hundreds of leading scientists as Coordinating Lead Authors and Lead Authors, and enlist hundreds more as Contributing Authors to provide complementary expertise in specific areas. IPCC reports undergo multiple rounds of drafting and review, ensuring the reports reflect the full range of views in the scientific community.
2. Reconstructing drought conditions, the study finds that the 2014 California drought was the most severe drought in the past twelve hundred years based on the Palmer Drought Severity Index, which estimates soil moisture (Nuccitelli 2014).
3. See Appendix Table 2 for a list of cyclone basins.
4. Category 5 storms are the most severe and refer to hurricanes with maximum sustained wind speeds exceeding 249 kilometers per hour.
5. The power dissipation index is defined as the integral over the lifetime of the event of its maximum surface wind speed cubed (Emanuel 2010).

3

The Rising Threat of Climate-Related Natural Disasters

Not only is it real, it's here, and its effects are giving rise to a frighten-ingly new global phenomenon: the man-made natural disaster.
—Barack Obama, President of the United States

The frequency of natural disasters recorded in the Emergency Events Database (EM-DAT 2015) has increased by almost threefold in the last four decades, from over thirteen hundred events in 1975–1984 to over thirty-nine hundred in 2005–2014 (figure 3.1). The sharp increase is seen only in hydrological and meteorological events.

Global

Over a million people worldwide have died from natural disasters since 2000, with damages estimated at over $1.7 trillion (EM-DAT 2015). Clear trends, however, are not expected in natural disaster impacts. A single Category 5 hurricane hitting New York, as with Sandy, would muddle trends and break existing records for damages. So would one extremely strong earthquake, as with the 2011 Tohoku earthquake and tsunami.

A look at the recent past shows the harsh blows of natural disasters.

- In 2011, estimates of global economic damages due to natural disasters ranged between $366 billion and $380 billion, making 2011 the costli-est year in terms of economic damages, with the Tohoku earthquake and tsunami incurring more than half of the losses (Munich Re 2012; Guha-Sapir et al. 2012).
- In 2012, climate-related events cost the global economy $160 billion, with $68 billion from Hurricane Sandy alone, making it the second costliest hurricane in United States history.

31

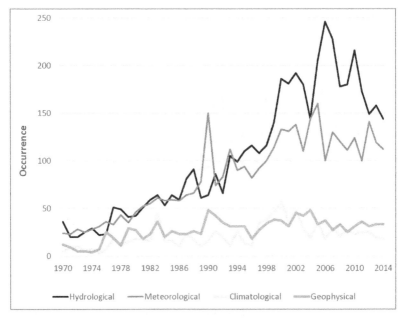

Figure 3.1. Global frequency of natural disasters by type, 1970–2014.

Source: Frequencies are authors' estimates based on data from the Emergency Event Database of the Center for Research on the Epidemiology of Disasters. http://www. emdat.be (accessed March 5, 2015).

- In 2013, Typhoon Haiyan wrought massive devastation in central Philippines, killing over seven thousand people.
- In 2014, natural disasters in Asia and the Pacific caused $59.6 billion in economic losses and claimed over six thousand lives (UNESCAP 2015).
- In 2015, Cyclone Pam ravaged Vanuatu, leaving one hundred thousand people, 40 percent of its population, in dire need of drinking water and seventy-five thousand without shelter (Prevention Web 2015b). In the same year, India's heatwave killed twenty-four hundred people (Prevention Web 2015a).

From 1970 to 2008, over 95 percent of deaths from natural disasters occurred in developing countries (IPCC 2012b). In the decade 2000–2009, the top forty humanitarian country recipients accounted for one-third of the number of global natural disasters and almost 80 percent of those killed (Kellet and Sparks 2012).

The number of people affected by natural disasters has also been increasing. This is particularly true for hydrological disasters. Prior to the 1990s, five-year averages did not reach fifty million people. This number doubled after the 1990s, and was mostly over a hundred million until 2014 (figure 3.2).

A decadal look at damages from natural disasters shows a steady increase in total damages worldwide. Damages from disasters translated roughly to $142 billion annually in the last ten-year period (2005–2014), a steep increase from the estimated annual damages of $36 billion two decades ago (1985–1994) (EM-DAT 2015).

In the last forty years, the damages in the United States due to natural disasters as a percentage of GDP have more than tripled. Its insurance losses from natural catastrophes rose from $16.1 billion in 2003 to $71.3 billion in 2012 (Baskin-Gerwitz 2013).

Without adaptive measures, disaster damages are expected to rise to $185 billion a year from economic and population growth alone (World Bank and United Nations 2010). Using probabilistic

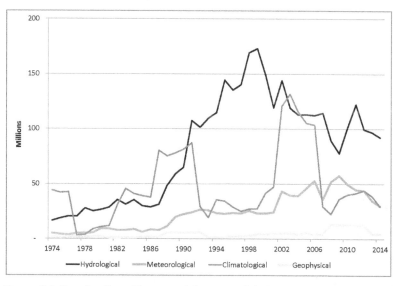

Figure 3.2. People affected by natural disasters: global trends, 1970–2014.

Note: This is based on the 5-year moving averages of the number of people affected a year. The cyclical spikes in number of people affected by climatological disasters is due to extreme droughts in India every 15 years.
Source: EM-DAT Database.

risk models, the global average annual loss from earthquakes, tsunami, cyclones, and flooding are now estimated at $314 billion—a figure greater than the annual GDPs of Pakistan, the Philippines, and Singapore. Roughly $120 billion of the total comes from Asia and the Pacific (UNISDR 2015a).

Asia and the Pacific

Asia and the Pacific accounted for 40 percent of the global frequency of natural disasters in the past forty-five years, three-quarters of which were hydrometeorological (figure 3.3). Since the turn of the millennium, the People's Republic of China, India, Indonesia, the Philippines, and the United States are among the top five countries most frequently struck by natural disasters. Resembling global trends, increasing occurrences of hydrological and meteorological disasters have been more pronounced in the region, compared to geophysical and climatological disasters.

Countries in Asia and the Pacific also top the lists of countries most vulnerable to climate change.[1] By 2025, it is expected that coastal populations at risk of flooding will increase to 410 million (from 300 million

Figure 3.3. Damage from the Asian Tsunami of 2004. *Aceh in northern Sumatra, Indonesia was virtually wiped off the map. At least 160,000 people died in and around the main city of Banda Aceh.*

Photo credit: ADB.

in 2010). Flooding will also affect inland populations in low-lying areas. From a group of fifty cities deemed most relevant to the global economy, Maplecroft (2014) identified five cities at extreme risk from climate change impacts. These are Dhaka, Mumbai, Manila, Kolkata, and Bangkok.

People Affected and Fatalities

During 1970–2014, 95 percent of all incidences of injury, homelessness, and other forms of deprivations of basic survival needs due to hydrological events were from Asia and the Pacific (figure 3.4). The comparable figure for meteorological events is 92 percent. High-income countries were least affected, with less than 1 percent of affected population coming from high-income countries.

Over ninety countries have at least 10 percent of their populations in areas with relatively high mortality risk from two or more hazards. Ten Asian countries have at least half their populations at risk, while Bangladesh and Nepal each have 97 percent of their populations at risk (Dilley et al. 2005).

Asia and the Pacific accounted for 55 percent of the 3.5 million lives that perished in natural disasters globally from 1970 to 2014. Within the region, over nine hundred thousand deaths were from earthquakes, over 750,000 from storms, and over two hundred thousand from floods (EM-DAT 2015).

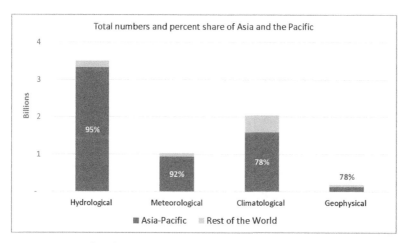

Figure 3.4. People affected by natural disasters: Worldwide, 1970–2014.

Source: EM-DAT Database.

Population growth in high-risk areas as well as poverty contribute to the region's vulnerability to disasters. From 1970 to 2014, almost two-thirds of deaths in the region from natural disasters were in low-income and lower-middle-income economies, with just 5 percent of deaths from high-income economies (UNESCAP 2014). Relative to country populations, low-income economies suffered eighty-six deaths per million population, while middle- and high-income countries suffered eleven or less deaths per million population (figure 3.5).

Economic Risk

Asia and the Pacific accounts for half of the world's losses from hydro-meteorological and geophysical disasters over the past forty years. Of global losses from earthquakes and other geophysical events, 75 percent were incurred in this region. In the same period, Asia and the Pacific incurred 63 percent of global economic losses from floods and other hydrological events. The Great East Japan Earthquake of 2011 was the costliest loss event worldwide during 1980–2013, while the

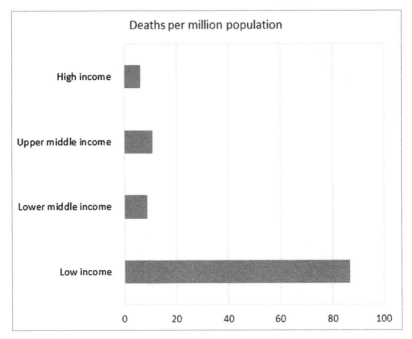

Figure 3.5. Deaths from natural disaster: Asia and the Pacific, 1970–2014.
Source: UNESCAP (2014).

Thailand floods, also in 2011, was the costliest flood event in this period. A quarter of global economic losses from meteorological events were incurred in Asia and the Pacific.

Disasters may cause greater absolute economic damage in high-income economies given their wealth and infrastructure, but lower-income economies are generally hit harder, losing a more significant portion of their GDP. The high- and upper-middle-income countries incurred 82 percent of the $1.3 trillion losses from disasters from 1970 to 2014 in the region. While the low-income countries shouldered less than 4 percent of this total; they were in a more precarious situation. The Pacific islands of Samoa and Vanuatu have had years when disasters completely wiped out their total annual output. In various years, losses from natural disasters surpassed national outputs of these low-income countries, with average losses amounting to 150 percent of GDP (figure 3.6) (UNESCAP 2014).

Of Typhoon Haiyan's destruction, only 7 percent of losses were insured. In comparison, of the estimated $15 billion losses from the 2013 floods in Central Europe, 20 percent were insured. Generally, less than 5 percent of disaster losses in Asia and the Pacific are insured

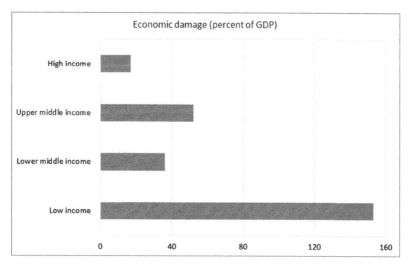

Figure 3.6. Economic impact of natural disasters: Asia and the Pacific, 1970–2014.

Note: GDP = gross domestic product.
Source: UNESCAP (2014).

compared to 40 percent in developed countries (Munich Re 2014). This makes losses more debilitating and rebuilding more draining.

The global average annual loss is concentrated in large and high-income economies exposed to cyclones, floods, and earthquakes. More than the absolute values of the average annual loss, the proportion relative to capital investments and social expenditure is more indicative of the threats a country faces for its development prospects. Disaster costs erode a significant proportion of capital investments or social spending and will also erode growth and social development potential.

For instance, the absolute multi-hazard average annual losses of Bangladesh, Cambodia, and the Philippines are small compared to those of the People's Republic of China, Japan, and the United States. But the bigger economies have the capacity to absorb and replenish capital stocks and spend for social development after disasters strike. The People's Republic of China's average annual loss of $31.9 billion is a mere 4 percent of social expenditure and less than 1 percent of its capital investments.

On the other hand, the Philippines' average annual loss of $7.9 billion, mostly attributable to cyclone risks, is equivalent to 69 percent of social expenditure and 14 percent of capital investments. For the Philippines, spending for the costs of future disasters can very well use up resources which should be going to education and health. The country also has the largest proportion of capital investment at risk from cyclones.

For flood risks, Myanmar's average annual loss exceeds its social expenditure. The country also has the largest proportion of capital investments at risk from floods. Small island states in the Pacific are also in very precarious situations. Vanuatu's average annual loss is equivalent to 76 percent of its social expenditure and 30 percent of capital investments.

Across regions, multi-hazard average annual loss is highest in East Asia and the Pacific, but the region also has the highest level of capital investment. The percentage of average annual loss to capital investments is less than 2 percent. South Asia on the other hand has the highest proportion of average annual loss for capital investments, at almost 5 percent.

Natural disasters have been increasingly destabilizing urban life. Disasters hitting cities have the potential to derail or cut heavily into economic growth, as they did in Thailand in 2011. It is estimated that flooding in that year cost the economy an estimated $46.5 billion in damages and production losses, and made the country's GDP contract by 13 percent (World Bank and GFDRR 2012). The floods were a stark illustration of how disasters can affect regional and global supply chains after flooding stopped production in computer and car factories.

A joint study by the World Bank, Asian Development Bank, and Japan International Cooperation Agency (2010) suggests that if current climate trends continue, flooding in vulnerable coastal cities in Asia is likely to occur more frequently by 2050. Costs from these events are projected to run into billions of US dollars, affecting the urban poor the most. Additional losses from climate change for a 1-in-30-year flood could reach $1.5 billion in Bangkok or 2 percent of its domestic product; in Manila additional costs could reach $0.65 billion or 6 percent of its domestic product.

Challenge for the Philippines

Typhoon Haiyan was the biggest humanitarian catastrophe of 2013. The Philippines, by various measures, is among the ten most vulnerable nations in the world, especially on climate change impacts. Ranked second in the United Nation's World Risk Index (2014), the country's location just north of the equator and west of the Northeast Pacific cyclone basin, puts it on the path of an average of twenty typhoons per year, six to nine of which make landfall.

An archipelago of over seventy-one hundred islands, the Philippines has one of the longest coastlines in the world, exposing its coastal populations to storm surges and sea level rise. Rapid and unmanaged urbanization contributes to this vulnerability, with 40 percent of the urban population living in slums. The country also ranks second highest in urban risk (UNU-EHS 2014)

The annual frequency of tropical cyclones in the Philippines does not show a notable change in trends, but the extent of damage and number of casualties are rising. It is no longer far-fetched to think that the country could see two events like 2009's Typhoon Ketsana in just one typhoon season.

Preparing for such scenarios means spending more and better ahead of disasters, investing in DRR and adaptation, and building capacity for relief and recovery. To meet these challenges, political leaders and economic managers need to be cognizant of the vital link between DRR and development and economic success. While there indeed is greater awareness today, it is arguable if this is commensurate with the degree of risks.

The economic losses caused by Typhoons Ketsana and Parma, which inundated much of the island of Luzon just days apart from each other in 2009, cost the Philippines some 2.7 percent of its GDP.[2] The typhoons led to the deaths of over a thousand people and pushed some half a million people into poverty (Government of the Philippines 2009).

Climate Trends in the Philippines

From 1971 to 2010, the Philippines experienced the highest frequency of intense meteorological disasters and the fourth highest frequency of intense hydrological disasters within Asia and the Pacific.[3] Climate data show that the intensity of extreme hydrometeorological hazards, the amount of daily rainfall, and maximum sustained winds associated with typhoons,[4] in the Philippines are rising.

Mean surface temperature anomalies have risen in the Philippines (figure 3.7), with annual means rising by 0.65°C during 1951–2010 (PAGASA n.d.). Higher temperature anomalies were concentrated after 1995.

The frequency of hot days (defined as days with maximum temperature greater than 30°C) increased in the past sixty years, and is projected to increase further, as will the number of days with

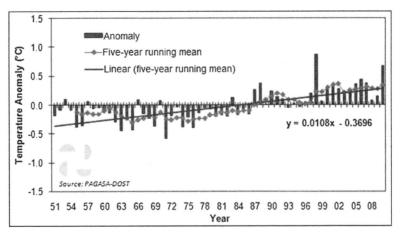

Figure 3.7. Annual mean surface temperature anomalies in the Philippines, 1951–2010.

Note: Temperature anomalies here represent departures from average temperature during 1971–2000.
Source: PAGASA.

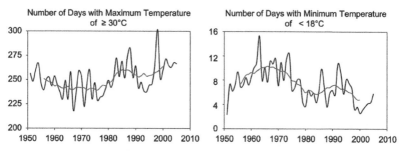

Figure 3.8. Frequency of hot days and cool days in the Philippines, 1950–2010.

Note: Annual frequency of occurrence days per station calculated from data taken at 28 observation stations. The black line shows the annual frequency of days per station. The gray line shows the 11-year running mean.
Source: Manila Observatory, with data from PAGASA.

maximum temperatures exceeding 35°C by 2020 (PAGASA n.d.). Cool days (defined as days with minimum temperature less than 18°C) are decreasing (figure 3.8).

There are no statistically significant trends in the frequencies of extreme daily rainfall, but it is projected that rainfall increases will be seen during the southwest and northeast monsoon seasons. From 2020 to 2050, heavy daily rainfall will become more frequent, especially in Luzon and the Visayas, while the number of dry days will increase in all parts of the country.

There is no clear trend showing high variability over the decades of the average number of tropical cyclones in the Philippines each year. But the number of strong typhoons with maximum sustained winds of 150 kilometers per hour and over during El Niño years has increased. And tropical cyclones of weaker intensity now have very intense associated rains.

Tropical cyclone paths have shifted southward, hitting areas not usually struck by typhoons. Figure 3.9 which shows the thirty-year running averages of the frequency of tropical cyclones passing over the Philippines indicates an increasing occurrence in the Visayas over the fifty-year period 1950–2000 (PAGASA n.d.). Tropical storms rarely cross Mindanao making its residents largely complacent and unprepared. With the devastation wrought by Typhoons Washi in 2011 and Bopha in 2012, Mindanao has dropped its claim of being typhoon-free (box 3.1).

The number of hot days is increasing, the frequency of strong typhoons has increased, and typhoon tracks have shifted. It has also

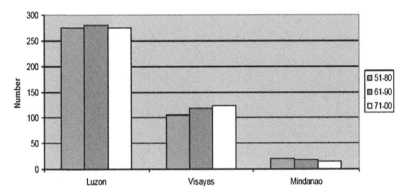

Figure 3.9. Decadal trends in tropical cyclone occurrence in the three main islands of the Philippines, 1951–2000.

Source: PAGASA.

been projected that the frequency of extreme daily rainfall will increase. These findings suggest heightened levels of risk and a move away from past trends. Risk reduction measures, disaster prevention, and climate adaptation will be necessary to protect the gains of development from this heightened risk.

Box 3.1. Mindanao: complacency and learning.

When Typhoons Washi in 2011 and Bopha in 2012 hit southern Philippines, residents of Mindanao were caught unaware and unprepared, leading to great loss of lives. Tracking the paths of typhoons of categories 3–5 in the Philippines, Typhoon Bopha was seen to be the lone strong typhoon to make landfall in Mindanao in the period 1990–2014. It appears that this unfamiliarity with storms constrained preventive action.

Typhoon Washi, though relatively weak, brought with it extreme precipitation and resulted in deadly floods and mudslides. But more than the rain, degraded forests and the complacency of both the residents and local authorities were blamed for the loss of some fourteen hundred lives, 670 from Cagayan de Oro alone. The typhoon ended up being the deadliest storm, globally, for 2011.

According to geologist Osin Sinsuat of the Mines and Geosciences Bureau, "our warnings were ignored . . . people need first-hand experience before they believe."

Cagayan de Oro learned its lesson well. In 2012, Typhoon Bopha followed a roughly similar track as Washi. This time Cagayan de Oro implemented preemptive evacuations. And while the city was placed under a state of calamity, it suffered a lone fatality.

Typhoon Bopha disrupted the lives and livelihoods of over six million people across thirty-four provinces, and killed some 1,900 people, mostly in Davao Oriental and Compostela Valley. And again, while typhoon warnings were given, residents who had no historical experience of typhoons did not believe the warnings.

According to Gibertz V. Luas, a farmer in Compostela Valley, "We were informed by local officials that a storm was coming, but knowing that my parents have lived here for a long time and no typhoon has ever been here, we disregarded the warnings."

Sources: ABS-CBN, IFRC 2013a, Interaksyon, ReliefWeb, Sun-Star.

Disaster Risk Reduction

There is far less complacency since Typhoon Ketsana struck Manila, the Philippines' economic hub and key metropolis, in September 2009. The depredations in the south caused by Typhoons Washi and Bopha show that the entire country– not just regions that were traditionally in the path of typhoons and tropical storms–is now more exposed to highly destructive storms.

Disaster awareness, weather forecasting, hazard mapping, and early warning systems in the Philippines are improving for the most part. Effective DRR and management involve all stakeholders, from the central and local governments down to the barangays (the smallest administrative division) and their residents.

The Philippine Geosciences and Mines Bureau's geohazard mapping program is identifying communities at risk from the landslides and flash floods so often triggered by seasonal typhoons and storms. A tablet computer recently developed by the Department of Science and Technology to provide barangay leaders with real-time weather and hazard information could become a critical decision-making tool for communities faced with approaching danger if produced in sufficient numbers.

The UN Office for Disaster Risk Reduction lauded the Philippines' DRR efforts, particularly its zero-casualty approach in handling

Typhoon Hagupit in 2014 which affected over 3.8 million people and effected a state of calamity in several provinces. In 2015, the Philippines was again praised for its success in reducing loss of life through its early warnings and organized evacuations as Typhoon Koppu lashed its 185 kph winds and inundated central and northern parts of Luzon.

The country needs more work on climate adaptation and significant investment to improve resilience to disasters. Urban and community planning and management must take center stage. Coastal cities such as Manila, with dense populations, investments and assets, are at risk. Climate-proofing these cities and building their resilience are necessary and urgent investments. Drainage systems need rehabilitating and water-carrying capacities expanded to cope with rising populations. Households living along waterways, and rivers and creeks, need to be transferred first before major flood control systems can be implemented. Persuading informal settlers to relocate has proved tough in the past. For the Philippines, upping the game in DRR and management is proving to be essential to securing the pace of economic growth and social progress in the years ahead.

Climate Action

Ensuring food and water security through investments in agriculture, adaptive technology, and sustainable practices are part of the country's Climate Change Action Plan. Even as the country remains a small contributor to global GHG emissions, national legislation and programs on renewable energy and cleaner transportation are being promoted.

Climate mitigation and a low-carbon path are in the Philippines' own interest. The local benefits of shifting to a low-carbon path include reduced energy costs through efficiency gains in buildings and manufacturing, reduced air pollution, and subsequently reduced public health risks from cleaner energy sources.

Fine particulate matter of ten microns or less in diameter generated by fossil-fuel combustion from vehicles, power plants, and industry is associated with cardiovascular and respiratory diseases, including asthma. While the World Health Organization did not set threshold levels for particulate matter, since these pollutants have health impacts even at low concentrations, they have set twenty micrograms per cubic meter (annual mean) as the guideline level. Manila recorded forty-seven micrograms per cubic meter in 2007 (WHO 2014b). Considering that cardiovascular diseases are the leading causes of mortality in the country, while respiratory diseases are the leading causes of morbidity, air pollution is a public health risk and should be a focus of action.

President Benigno Aquino's call for timely global response is clear recognition of the problem. Without waiting for the bigger economies and biggest emitters to act, or for global agreements, the Philippines' unilateral decision to tackle climate change with its own resources will eventually be to its own advantage. Programs to improve disaster resilience, for example, through re-greening forests, will benefit local communities and help minimize local flooding. Low-carbon energy will reduce pollution and sustainable mass transport will be more inclusive.

Notes

1. The lists included in this study are based on different sets of criteria. World Risk Report 2014 ranked 171 countries based on (i) exposure to hazards; (ii) susceptibility; (iii) coping capacity; and (iv) adaptive capacity (UNU-EHS 2014). The Germanwatch Global Climate Risk Index 2015 ranked 181 countries based on historical data of deaths and losses from 1994 to 2013 from weather-related loss events (Kreft et al. 2014). Maplecroft's Climate Change Vulnerability Index 2015 ranked 198 countries based on the risk of exposure to climate change and extreme events, the current human sensitivity to that exposure, and the capacity of a country to adapt to or take advantage of the potential impacts of climate change (Maplecroft 2014).

2. Luzon is the country's biggest island and is considered as its economic heartland.

3. Countries with much larger land area topped the list in hydrological disasters: PRC, India, and Indonesia.

4. A typhoon is a tropical cyclone in the northwestern Pacific Ocean with sustained winds of at least 119 kilometers per hour.

4

Climate Change Mitigation

No national leader in the history of humanity has ever faced this question. Will we survive or will we disappear under the sea?
—Enele Sopoaga, Prime Minister of Tuvalu

Unless GHG emissions, including CO_2 concentrations, are checked, increases in average global temperatures will continue and climate change risks will escalate. The shift to renewable energy, improvements in energy efficiency, and limiting deforestation are all climate change mitigation measures which will help reduce GHG emissions and the accompanying risks. Given the substantial time delay between GHG emissions reductions and the actual reduction in atmospheric GHG concentrations, and the irreversibility of climate change on a multi-century time scale, it is imperative that mitigation actions start now.

It should be in a country's interest to pursue climate action soonest. If countries ignore climate change now, the cost of tackling them in the future will be many times greater. For instance, a ten-year delay in climate mitigation will require the annual rate of decline in CO_2 emissions to be twice as fast to stabilize its atmospheric concentration (Stern and Noble 2008).

GHGs stay in the atmosphere for a long time. Elevated levels of GHG concentrations and surface air temperatures will remain elevated for hundreds of years. Regardless of mitigation, global warming of close to 1.5°C above pre-industrial levels is already locked into the Earth's atmospheric system. Adaptation measures must be in place to minimize the negative impact of this warmer climate on agriculture and food security, to reduce disaster risks on urban and rural infrastructure, and to limit interruptions in commercial, industrial, and financial operations. Climate adaptation will help reduce risks in the near term, even as global warming and the associated impacts of climate change continue.

Figure 4.1 illustrates how climate change mitigation and adaptation can reduce the cost of climate change impacts. While mitigation should continue its traditional focus on reducing GHG emissions, increasing carbon sinks, and switching to low-carbon energy, adaptation should occur simultaneously to accommodate and readjust to the reality of changing environments and intensifying hazards. By doing both climate mitigation and adaptation, costs of climate change impacts can be reduced, major catastrophes avoided, and irreversible damage prevented. With no climate action, growth will stall and the cost of climate change impacts will be unacceptable.

But figure 4.1 has a more crucial point: while the need for adaptation cannot be overemphasized, climate adaptation without climate mitigation will be futile. Without mitigation, impacts of climate change will be most extreme and severe that no amount of adaptation and preparedness can protect lives, communities, and economies.

With a quarter of global emissions coming from energy supply, reducing the carbon intensity of electricity generation, also called

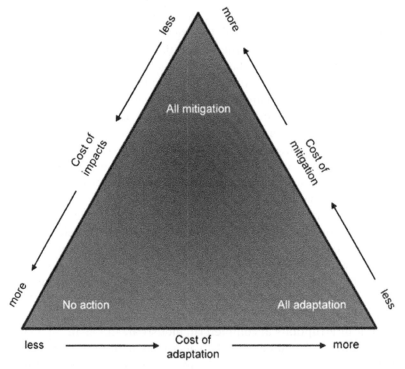

Figure 4.1. Mitigation and adaptation.

Source: IPCC (2012).

decarbonization, is a key element in mitigation (figure 4.2). Unless carbon intensities in energy production are significantly reduced, emission levels from this sector are projected to almost double (or even triple) by 2050 from 2010 levels. To limit CO_2 levels to 450 ppm, 80percent of electricity will have to be supplied by renewables and nuclear by 2050, and CO_2 capture and storage will have to be employed by all fossil-fuel power generation by 2100 (IPCC 2014b). Trends will have to be reversed—from 1990 to 2012 CO_2 emissions from electricity and heat almost doubled from a surge in coal use.

Aside from electricity and heat generation, energy use and fossil-fuel combustion in transport, buildings, and industry contribute to energy emissions. With energy emissions comprising two-thirds of global GHG emissions, mitigation measures should zoom in on energy, especially fossil fuels which still account for over 80 percent of world energy supply, and coal combustion which generated the largest share of CO_2 emissions in 2012.

In the transport sector, CO_2 emissions from road, marine, and aviation bunker fuel combustion all grew by at least 60 percent since

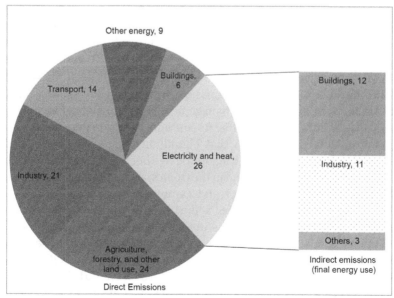

Figure 4.2. Greenhouse gas emissions share by economic sector, 2010.
Source: IPCC (2014b).

the 1990s. But with road transport accounting for three quarters of transport emissions, a transformation of the urban and rural transport systems is needed. Low-carbon mass transport, a shift away from urban sprawls and the car culture, and well-planned compact cities would need time and infrastructure investments. These investments will not only be good for climate, but would also contribute to economic efficiency and quality living.

Including indirect emissions, the industry sector accounts for some 32 percent of GHG emissions. Upgrading and the use of more efficient technologies to improve energy efficiency can substantially reduce the sector's CO_2 emissions. Reduction of methane, nitrous oxide and fluorinated gas is another important mitigation opportunity for industry (IPCC 2014b).

As a result of the Montreal Protocol which removed the use of ozone depleting chlorofluorocarbons (CFCs) and hydrochlorofluorocarbons (HCFCs), the use of hydrofluorocarbons (HFCs) as refrigerants, aerosol propellants, solvents, and fire retardants has been increasing rapidly since the 1990s at a rate of 10-15 percent a year (Global Commission on the Economy and Climate 2015). Unfortunately HFCs are potent GHGs, with long atmospheric lifetimes (at over 200 hundred years) and high global warming potentials (ten thousand times more than CO_2). Replacing HFCs with refrigerants with lower global warming potentials, deployment of improved technology to reduce emissions, and incorporating the phase down of HFCs into the Montreal Protocol are mitigation options to pursue.

Another quarter of emissions are from the agriculture, forestry, and other land-use sectors. While emissions from this sector are projected to decline, sustainable forest management and reducing deforestation remain relevant efforts since forests continue to be threatened. Satellite data from 2000 to 2012 show that 2.3 million square kilometers (nine times the size of the United Kingdom) have been lost from the world's forests, with a continuing trend in the tropics, such as in Angola, Bolivia, Indonesia, Malaysia, Paraguay, and Zambia (Hansen et al. 2013).

Across regions, Asia and the Pacific has emerged as the world's biggest contributor of CO_2 emissions, at over 40 percent in 2010 (figure 4.3). With increasing population, gross domestic product (GDP) per capita, and CO_2 intensity of energy consumption, Asia and the Pacific emissions grew by 330 percent from 1970 to 2010 (IPCC 2014b).

For every 1 percent of economic growth, there is an associated 1 percent increase in GHG emissions (World Bank-IEG 2009).

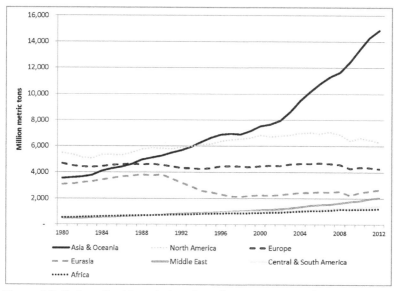

Figure 4.3. Carbon dioxide emissions from the consumption of energy by region.

Note: Regional classification used is that of the US Energy Information Administration.
Source: US Energy Information Administration.

However, there are various examples of activities and policies that can promote growth while limiting GHG emissions. Climate action encourages a shift to high value-added production modes, which can boost the credit rating of businesses and governments. There are examples of carbon sink expansions through business-friendly forestry projects. More generally, opportunities exist to use sound environmental policies to promote rather than hinder economic development.

As technological and government disincentives are reduced, large-scale corporations are stepping up the search for renewable energy. The steady growth in renewables and energy efficiency markets indicates business potential that must be appreciated and reached.

The Carbon Disclosure Project, an investor-led initiative that helps countries generate returns through carbon reducing and energy efficiency projects, engaged 300 companies from high emitting industries[1] to report emission reductions and investment returns on carbon reduction activities. Based on the performance of 241 companies which responded, carbon reduction projects generated an internal rate of return of 33.6 percent, while reducing emissions by 169 million metric tonnes CO_2 (Carbon Disclosure Project 2014). These high rates of return should have propelled investments in low-carbon and energy efficiency projects, yet investments in climate action continue to be inadequate.

From 2010 to 2013, the world's five hundred largest businesses continued to increase emissions by 3 percent (Thomson Reuters 2014). Christiana Figueres of the United Nations Framework Convention on Climate Change has urged businesses to take climate action into their own hands, and not to wait for policy changes or government initiatives, but rather help push policy toward climate action.

The World Economic Outlook's Special Report on Climate Change (2015) focuses on five energy measures to help achieve an earlier peak in GHG emissions based on proven technologies and policies: improving energy efficiency in buildings, industry, and transport; phasing out inefficient coal-fired power plants; increasing investments in renewables; removing fossil-fuel subsidies; and reducing methane from oil and gas production.

The 2015 New Climate Economy Report further asserts that climate change can be overcome. Aside from action on clean energy, low-carbon cities and restoration of degraded lands and forests can already fill in at least 82 percent of the emissions gap—the reduction in GHG emissions needed to keep global warming under 2°C. The success of climate action depends on the consistency of policies and the scaling-up of actions through the involvement of both developed and developing countries, governments and businesses, investors and communities.

Implementation of policy, and scaling-up of investments in climate mitigation efforts will entail costs. Annual global climate finance flows in 2013 are estimated at $331 billion, about $28 billion below the 2012 levels (Buchner et al. 2014). The overall decrease is mainly due to falling cost of some renewable energy technologies. One key issue remains: would these efforts be sufficient to deliver low-carbon energy systems and limit carbon concentrations to 450 ppm?

The other question is: would the funds committed under the COP21 agreement be enough to tide over developing countries in their transition toward low-carbon and climate-resilient economies? In 2013, $52.2 billion was mobilized for this purpose, 25 percent of which came from the private sector. Almost the same pattern was seen in 2014. Over a quarter of the \$61.8 billion was from private finance mobilized by bilateral and multilateral channels (OECD 2015).

Carbon Pricing

Experts argue that the dual objective of climate mitigation and spurring economic growth can be achieved by imposing a price on CO_2 emissions that reflects the burden it imposes on the environment. Ottmar Edenhofer, an adviser to the New Climate Economy Report (2014), said: "Economic growth and emissions reductions can be achieved together... Pricing CO_2 is key" (Harvey 2014).

Since emitters do not bear the costs of the damages caused by GHG emissions, Nicholas Stern, co-chair of the New Climate Economy Report, goes further, saying that this is the largest market failure that the world has ever seen, and that carbon pricing, which corrects for this externality, is the "most urgent policy" today. Akerlof (2014) even suggested to place a uniform tax on carbon emissions that would escalate until emissions fall to desirable levels.

Two key approaches in carbon pricing have been advocated. First is imposing a carbon tax which effectively sets a price on carbon, where carbon emission savings cannot be determined upfront. And second, carbon trading where the emission savings are based on allocated emission quotas while the market determines the carbon price. Either way, the intended effect is to reduce demand for high-carbon emitting fossil fuels and increase demand for renewable sources and lower-emission fuels (such as natural gas). Putting a price on carbon emissions can persuade energy companies, power generators, and consumers to act in environmentally responsible ways.

Carbon taxes have been traditionally opposed by fossil-fuel producers. However, in recent months, top executives of six large European oil and gas companies called for a tax on carbon emissions, as they realize the need for governments to provide clear and stable frameworks that help stimulate low-carbon development. Energy prices should reflect the damage caused by emissions, especially in energy-intensive countries such as the People's Republic of China and the United States. A higher price of carbon will boost the confidence of those investing in or converting to carbon-reducing technologies. This will require credible scientific institutions to demonstrate how productivity and climate change mitigation can be reconciled.

In the economic downturn following the global financial crisis of 2008, carbon prices on the European Emissions Trading System plunged from about €25 per tonne in 2008 to less than €5 per tonne. Failure to reduce emission allowances (quotas) as economic slowdown occurred is a major cause. In general, it may be worth trying to limit carbon prices within a narrow band as in the California cap-and-trade regime.

Getting decision-makers to adopt a carbon tax has been difficult. In Australia, the newly elected conservative government repealed the carbon tax in September 2014. This repeal clearly shows how economic concerns can overshadow and complicate efforts to combat climate change, and sets back plans for countries to knit together markets for trading emission quotas.

Governments that introduce carbon pricing would need to safeguard local industry from imported goods from countries where an equivalent carbon-pricing regime is not in place. To what extent this would impinge upon existing trade agreements is a matter of conjecture.

Imposing carbon taxes on fossil fuels is one policy for curbing CO_2 emissions that is administratively quick and easy to implement, and can be easily combined with other policy options. Compared with other policy options for carbon mitigation, such as cap-and-trade, control regulations, and subsidies for renewable energy, carbon taxes are more administratively effective. Carbon taxes may also improve the financial viability of contemporary technological strategies and climate change solutions. An important first step is information and advocacy. While easy to implement, popular support is necessary.

Removing Fossil-Fuel Subsidies

Economists have tagged carbon taxes as a win-win strategy for cleaner air, lower deficits, and drive-clean technology. The other side of this coin, with the same win-win upshots, is scrapping fossil-fuel subsidies—a measure that is good for the economy and environmental sustainability. Estimated to be responsible for over a third of GHG emissions in the past three decades, subsidies are introducing inefficiencies and diverting funds away from hospitals, schools, and cleaner energy. Phasing out inefficient and costly fuel subsidies is a step that countries everywhere must take, especially economies with bigger carbon footprints.

Asian economies, in general, have higher energy subsidies than the rest of the world. Pretax subsidies—the difference between domestic and world energy prices—are 0.9 percent of Asia's GDP. Post-tax subsidies, which include externality charges such as lost taxes and damage to other economic sectors, are approximately 4.4 percent of GDP (Petri and Thomas 2013).

Globally, fossil-fuel subsidies were estimated to be over $500 billion in 2013 (IEA 2014). This estimate rockets tenfold if the environmental damage from energy consumption is incorporated. In 2013, this amounted to some $4.9 trillion (or 6.5 percent of global GDP) and is projected to reach $5.3 trillion in 2015 (Coady et al. 2015).

Fossil-fuel subsidies encourage GHG emissions and discourage investments in clean energy. Energy subsidies also impose huge fiscal costs, crowding out other public spending, such as in education and health. If energy subsidies are removed, it is estimated that global CO_2 emissions can be cut by more than 20 percent, and air pollution deaths cut by more than half. Globally, eliminating post-tax fossil-fuel subsidies in 2015 could also raise government revenue by $2.9 trillion (3.6 percent of global GDP) (Coady et al. 2015).

Fossil-fuel subsidies are also highly regressive, as they tend to benefit the richer segments of the population rather than the poor. A larger portion of the subsidies will accrue to those with higher energy consumption levels, such as the urban middle classes with larger vehicles and more appliances. In Mexico, 80 percent of electricity subsidies for irrigation went to the richest 10 percent of farmers (Global Commission on the Economy and Climate 2014).

While removing fossil-fuel subsidies would be a step toward reducing inequality, measures to phase these out have also seen strong opposition from the lower income groups. Higher energy prices will impact meager budgets more. Subsidy reforms should be accompanied by targeted pro-poor spending and cash transfer payments which will benefit poorer households more.

As oil prices declined in 2014, India and Malaysia seized the opportunity and cut fossil-fuel subsidies, while Indonesia entirely scrapped subsidies for petrol in January 2015. With this move, Indonesia will have some $16 billion in savings to spend on health, education, and infrastructure—spending which is expected to improve the country's longer-term prospects. Malaysia went a step further by directly channeling its subsidy savings on cash transfer schemes for the poor.

Renewable Energy

Considered one of the most promising mitigation approaches, the development of renewable energy sources bypasses problems associated with taxes and excessive government regulations.

Although there is no one-to-one correlation between the increase in the share of renewable energy in electricity generation and a fall in global GHG emissions, progress in renewable energy development is promising.

Since 1980, renewable energy in electricity generation tripled from 1.7 trillion kilowatt-hours to 4.7 trillion kilowatt-hours in 2012 (US EIA). Figure 4.4 shows that the steepest increase was in Asia and the Pacific where it grew almost sixfold. In 2013, the share of renewables to total energy generation worldwide increased to 8.5 percent—preventing some 1.2 billion tonnes of CO_2 from being released (Frankfurt School-UNEP/BNEF 2015). Fossil fuels continue to dominate, but the situation could change.

In 2012, renewable energy, mostly hydroelectric, accounted for over a fifth of total global electricity production. In Latin America, the almost two-thirds share of hydropower pushed the share of fossil fuels to less than a third. In Europe, the combined share of nuclear and renewables accounts for more than half of electricity generation. Electricity generation in Asia and the Pacific and North America continue to be dependent on fossil fuels, with 78 percent and 63 percent

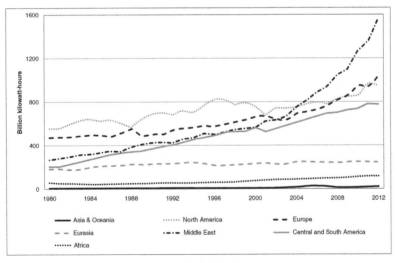

Figure 4.4. Renewable electricity net generation by region, 1980–2012.

Note: Regional classification used is that of the US Energy Information Administration.
Source: US Energy Information Administration.

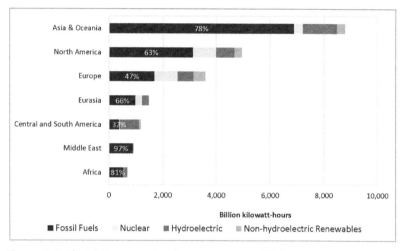

Figure 4.5. Electricity generation by energy source, 2012.

Note: Percentages show share of electricity generated using fossil fuel per region. Regional classification used is that of the US Energy Information Administration.
Source: US Energy Information Administration.

shares, respectively (figure 4.5). These two regions are also the biggest consumers of electricity—their combined consumption makes up 64 percent of the worldwide total. A transformation in these two regions is necessary to make some headway in global mitigation efforts.

Global investments in renewable energy grew by over 30 percent in 2010, and a further 18 percent in 2011, despite the economic slowdown in the West. This was followed, however, by two consecutive years of contraction, which reduced investments by as much as 17 percent in 2013 from 2011 levels (figure 4.6).

Renewable energy rebounded in 2014, even with falling oil prices. Investments reached $270 billion globally, up 17 percent from 2013's $232 billion. The major impetus of the 2014 surge came from the People's Republic of China and Japan, which together were responsible for half of the $150 billion investments in solar energy. In Europe, renewable investments were boosted by headway in offshore wind investments.

While the 2014 renewable investment levels are only the second highest, from the 2011 record of $279 billion, 2014 investments installed

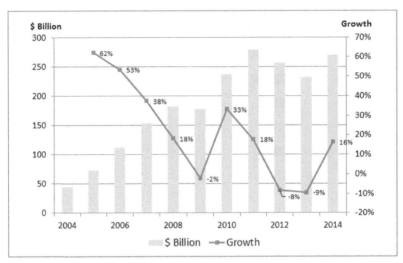

Figure 4.6. Global trends in renewable energy investment, 2004–2014.

Source: Frankfurt School-UNEP/Bloomberg New Energy Finance (2015a).

more energy capacity. Due to the declining capital and technological costs of renewables, particularly for wind and solar, more energy capacity was installed for each billion US dollars invested. In 2014, 130 gigawatts power capacity was installed (ninety-five gigawatts from wind and solar), compared to the eighty gigawatts of capacity installed in 2011 (Frankfurt School-UNEP/BNEF 2015).

Costs of generating electricity from renewables have seen sharp decreases since 2009, such that levelized costs of electricity from solar photovoltaics and onshore wind in some regions can already compete with conventional coal plants. The global average levelized cost of solar photovoltaic electricity went down by some 60 percent from $315 per MWh in 2009 to $122 per MWh in 2015 (figure 4.7). In the People's Republic of China, levelized cost of onshore wind electricity at seventy-seven dollar per MWh is now lower than that of combined-cycle gas turbine at $113 per MWh, but still higher than coal fired at forty-four dollars per MWh. Onshore wind electricity costs in Germany and the United Kingdom are now lower than both gas and coal (Frankfurt School-UNEP/BNEF 2015; BNEF 2015a, 2015b).

The International Energy Agency (IEA) estimated that in 2015, 90 percent of all new electricity growth globally came from renewable sources with over 50 percent attributable to wind energy. This signifies a significant shift away from fossil fuels. These improvements in energy efficiency were key to keeping energy-related CO_2 emissions flat from 2013 through 2015. IEA data also showed a decoupling of GHG emissions from economic growth.

Costs of renewables are expected to go down further. By 2020, estimates for the People's Republic of China and the United States show that producing electricity from both onshore wind and large solar plants will come out cheaper compared to gas and coal. The increasing competitiveness of wind and solar, with the right mix of regulations and incentives should help ensure the strength of this industry.

The People's Republic of China provides an example of a policy-led development in renewable energy that has created jobs, income, and revenue streams for nascent low-carbon industries (box 4.1).

While Germany will likely generate almost 80 percent of its electricity from renewables by 2050, developing countries may face roadblocks.

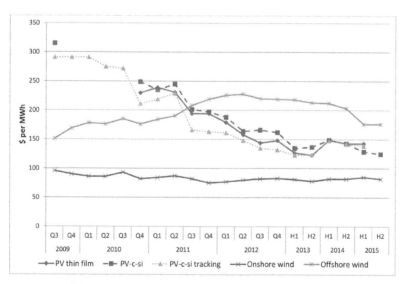

Figure 4.7. Global average levelized cost of electricity.

Notes: PV=Photovoltaic; PV-c-si= crystalline silicon photovoltaics; PV-c-si tracking=sun-tracking crystalline silicone photovoltaic.
Sources: Frankfurt School-UNEP/BNEF 2015; BNEF 2015.

Short-term business uncertainties, political ambivalence, government austerity, and competitive pressures from industries such as shale gas could slow investments in renewables. Because of the unique situation in many developing countries, companies will have to take extra risk-taking, innovation, and experimenting to make the shift to renewables.

In Asia, the private sector's potential in promoting environmentally sustainable and affordable solar and wind energy is promising. Private investments in India and Thailand in particular have made strides in solar and wind energy generation.

Box 4.1. Mitigation by decree: the case of the People's Republic of China.

The People's Republic of China's Renewable Energy Law offers a variety of financial incentives for energy sector development, such as a national fund to foster renewable energy development and discounted lending and preferential tax treatment for renewable energy projects. The People's Republic of China also requires its power grid operators to purchase resources only from registered renewable energy producers. These policies and financial incentives have encouraged major advances in wind power, as well as, solar power development, and have created more jobs.

To directly encourage joint ventures and local technology transfers in large wind turbine technology, the People's Republic of China mandated the use of locally made wind turbines. Through the Ministry of Science and Technology, the country has subsidized wind energy research and development expenditure since 1996. From 2005 to 2009, the country's generating capacity expanded by over 100 percent annually.

By 2009, the People's Republic of China was the world's largest solar photovoltaic cell manufacturer, producing 45 percent of the global supply. It is now the world's largest market for solar hot water, accounting for nearly two-thirds of global capacity. More than 10 percent of Chinese households rely on the sun to heat their water.

Zhangbei (Hebei) Windpower Project (left) and solar panels in Guangdong Energy Efficiency and Environment Improvement Project (right)

Photo credit: ADB.

Direct financing of renewable energy by the public has emerged as a promising approach. Crowdfunding of solar panels through an online platform allows small, nonaccredited investors to earn interest in financing clean energy projects. Mosaic, the company that introduced this service, raised $1.1 million for a dozen solar projects within three months. But as large international financial organizations are not structured to pursue such initiatives, private individuals and corporations need to be encouraged to invest in these emerging mitigation markets.

Nuclear Energy

While safety and security concerns over its use are intense, nuclear energy has the potential to contribute to bringing about the type of clean energy mix that will be required to scale back on the global dependence on fossil fuels. Nuclear power compares favorably with other renewable energy options in terms of GHG emissions, air pollution, and cost efficiency. The IPCC estimates the median value of emissions from nuclear plants at sixteen grams of CO_2-equivalent per kilowatt hour, about as much as a wind turbine and far less than fossil-fuel plants. The IEA notes that nuclear power is one of the world's largest sources of low-carbon energy with an average output equivalent to that of four thousand windmills.

The IPCC puts nuclear power at par with renewables among the low-carbon energy sources whose share of electricity generation must grow to 80 percent by 2050 if global warming is to be capped at 2°C over pre-Industrial Revolution levels. France relies heavily on nuclear power. Its state-controlled electricity utility Électricité de France (EDF) says nearly 98 percent of its power was free of carbon emissions in 2014. EDF says its emissions amounted to seventeen grams of CO_2-equivalent per kilowatt hour, which is twenty times less than the European average, and reduced CO_2 emissions by thirteen million tons, or 21 percent, in 2014 by reducing power generation from fossil-fuel plants in favor of nuclear power.

However, the IPCC acknowledges the need to find acceptable responses to fears over safety, waste disposal, and proliferation of nuclear weapons. Public concerns about nuclear safety came in the wake of the Fukushima meltdown in 2011. Additional public concerns also exist over the handling and disposal of radioactive waste and other associated risks. And the expansion of nuclear power creates worries about the proliferation of nuclear weapons. While new generations of nuclear power promise to reduce these risks, public opinion and geopolitical considerations will undoubtedly be key in determining the future of nuclear power in the world.

Energy Efficiency

With the appropriate mix of policies and technology, energy efficiency could be a key driver of lower fuel consumption, and consequently lower emissions. Using less energy through better efficiency to deliver transport, communication, lighting, and cooling and heating services has contributed sizably to the reduction of GHG emissions. It is not only new cars that consume less fuel. New buildings also consume four to ten times less energy than twenty-year-old buildings.

Energy efficiency improvements in eleven of the twenty-nine-member countries of the International Energy Agency contributed to savings of 1,336 million tons of oil equivalent in 2011, equivalent to almost 60 percent of total final consumption of these countries.[2] Fuel saved exceeded the 2011 total consumption of the European Union and Asia (excluding the People's Republic of China) (OECD-IEA 2014). If they had not improved energy efficiency, Group of Twenty (G20) countries would be consuming 32 percent more energy today (Creuheras 2015).

With energy efficiency capable of displacing a whole continent's fuel needs, the International Energy Agency dubs it the "first fuel." As such, the efficacy of energy efficiency in price stability, energy security, sustainable development, and climate change mitigation must not be dismissed.

Energy efficiency progressed steadily during the past decade, with over $300 billion in investments in 2012—higher than those in renewable energy in the same year and even higher than in conventional coal, oil, and gas electricity. Energy service companies are growing and are now worth $56 billion in Europe, $12 billion in the People's Republic of China, and $6.5 billion in the United States (The Economist 2015b).[3]

Energy intensity must be reduced at a rate of 2.9 percent a year until 2035 if global warming is to be limited to 2°C. This is almost twice the 1.6 percent reduction a year from 2005 to 2014 (OECD-IEA 2014).

Experts see much potential for energy efficiency in the emerging markets, especially in transport, with light-duty vehicles in non-OECD countries presenting the biggest opportunity. Driven by vehicle fuel economy standards, energy efficiency investments in vehicles are estimated to reach $80 billion annually and will save some $40 to $190 billion in fuel costs (OECD-IEA 2014). This push for efficiency must also include heavy-duty vehicles, which have a growing share in freight energy consumption.

Energy demand in the buildings sector is expected to double due to rising wealth, lifestyle changes, housing, and urbanization. This will raise GHG emissions of the sector by 50 percent to 150 percent by 2050 (IPCC 2014b). With buildings' long lifespans, the speedy adoption of very low-energy building codes, and the retrofitting of building stocks would produce substantial energy savings, reducing emissions substantially: retrofitting buildings can reduce heating and cooling energy use by 50 percent to 90 percent.

Forest Management and Protection

Reducing and preventing deforestation is the mitigation option with the largest and most immediate carbon stock impact per hectare a year globally, according to the IPCC. Deforestation is held accountable for 20 percent–24 percent of global GHG emissions. Even as some studies revise this share to about 12 percent (within a 6 percent–17 percent range), the role of securing forests in climate change mitigation remains significant (Lang 2009). While use of fossil fuels dominates GHG emissions, stabilizing global temperatures and climate systems will be practically impossible without reducing emissions from the forest sector.

Some studies even indicate that cutting down forests has a more direct effect on climate—that deforestation is more than just reducing the Earth's carbon sink and releasing CO_2 into the atmosphere. Scientists have observed that deforestation in the Amazon has been accompanied by widespread decreases in forest transpiration, changes in cloud and rain dynamics, and an extended duration of the dry season (Phillips 2014).

Preventing deforestation as a climate mitigation strategy also presents an economy-boosting opportunity. But continued deforestation suggests that stopping it is not without intricacies and stumbling blocks.

Global deforestation numbers suggest a losing battle. For some thirty developing countries, including Bolivia, Brazil, Indonesia, Myanmar, and Zambia, deforestation and forest degradation continue to be the

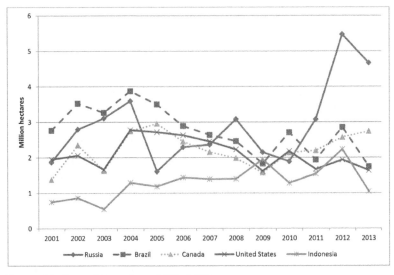

Figure 4.8. Annual forest loss, 2001–2013.

Source: Hansen (2013).

dominant source of CO_2 emissions (Lang 2009). Countries with the most expansive forests—Brazil, Canada, Indonesia, the Russian Federation, and the United States—are also losing the most, with Indonesia losing its forests the fastest (figure 4.8). These five countries accounted for more than 60 percent of global forest loss from 2000 to 2012. And while deforestation is being reduced in some areas, it continues elsewhere. Brazil's reduction in deforestation was offset by increasing forest loss in Angola, Indonesia, Malaysia, Paraguay, Bolivia, and Zambia (Hansen et al. 2013).

Commercial agriculture, responsible for 40 percent of total forest clearing, is the major driver of deforestation (Hosonuma et al. 2012). Latin American forests are being cleared for soy fields and cattle ranches, and the tropical forests of Indonesia and Malaysia for palm oil plantations (box 4.2). In less-developed regions such as Africa, local and subsistence agriculture account for most of forest clearing. Forests are cleared for urban expansion in the United States and for tar sands development in Canada. In a nutshell, forests are being cleared in response to local and global market signals and dynamics. As such, forest management and conservation policies should strongly involve economic forces.

The growing markets for soy, palm oil, and cattle are as unstoppable as urbanization. However, economic evidence also reveals that a healthy natural resource base is necessary to sustain development gains. More importantly, there should be no trade-off between environmental protection and economic development and poverty alleviation. For instance, forest economic valuations in Panama and Zambia indicate the absence of any clear economic rationale for continued deforestation. Panama loses $300 million a year from deforestation while Zambia's forests contribute as much as 4.7 percent to the country's GDP and provide over a million jobs (UNEP 2014).

Forest ecosystems will remain forested as long as the true value of forest products and services are recognized and incorporated into economic decisions. For as long as this economic value is greater than that of alternative land uses, conversion to other land uses can be discouraged. Establishing that land is worth more with trees than without is important. The challenge is in finding the correct valuation of intangible and unpriced goods and services such as clean air and water, biodiversity, sustainable livelihoods, and prevention of GHG emissions.

From Brazil, the largest economy in Latin America, to Indonesia, the largest in Southeast Asia, ranchers and loggers routinely cut a hectare of forest to create a pasture worth a few hundred US dollars, releasing hundreds of tons of CO_2 into the atmosphere. Again, establishing that forested land is worth more is one mutually beneficial solution. At prices of $10 for every ton of unreleased emissions, those groves could generate several times more from carbon markets than from pasture or deforestation.

The Reduced Emissions from Deforestation and Degradation (REDD+) agenda under the aegis of the United Nations Framework Convention on Climate Change offers developing countries incentives to reduce deforestation and strengthen conservation and sustainable management of forests. By putting a price on avoided deforestation, or on ensuring that forests remain forests, REDD+ helps protect forest areas and the local environment, while meeting local income generation goals.

Box 4.2. The catastrophe of Indonesia's forest fires.

Every year for the past eighteen years, large tracts of plantations and forests in Indonesia are burned to clear the way for paper and pulp, and palm oil plantations. Every year, the pollution and haze from the fires make people sick and disrupt schools across Southeast Asia. Among the thousands that fled Pekanbaru in Riau Province, Indonesia to escape the hazardous smoke is Greenpeace blogger Zamzami. And he writes, "My wife and daughter should be at our home in Pekanbaru . . . it's been more than a month since we . . . escaped to my parent's house in West Sumatra. But like a dark cloud over my head I've since discovered that wherever I go, smoke follows." (2015)

Various studies have shown how costly these annual forest fires are, yet slash and burn practice is still mistakenly seen as the most cost effective way to clear forests. The worst case of burning was in 1997 when six million hectares of forests and peatlands were razed and burned, with estimated losses amounting to some $20.1 billion (Varma, 2003). The Center for International Forest Research estimates that forestry and farming losses were around $8.5 billion, while losses from short-term health impacts and tourism amounted to $4.5 billion (CIFOR 2015). In 2015 alone, half a million cases of acute respiratory tract infections in Kalimantan and Sumatra have been attributed to people's exposure to smoke from burning forests (Lamb 2015). This is not surprising since Pollutant Standard Indices (PSI) in the worst- affected areas go over 2000 PSI, when 300 PSI levels are already hazardous. And while the resulting haze is worst for those nearest, the hazardous air reaches as far as Kuala Lumpur in Malaysia, Phuket in Thailand, and Singapore.

Counting the economic losses across the region from health costs, closing of schools and businesses, and cancelled flights, it becomes apparent that forest burning is most costly. Including its devastating effect to the environment and climate makes the picture direr.

Carbon emission estimates from the 1997 fires range from 0.81 to 2.59 gigatonnes, equivalent to as much as 13 percent–40 percent of the entire world's annual fossil-fuel emissions (Page et al. 2002). With the long dry season and the strong El Niño of 2015, the year's forest and peat fires are on track to match 1997 having released 0.6 gigatonnes as of September (NASA Earth Observatory 2015). These numbers already rival that of United Kingdom's and Germany's yearly emissions (Carrington 2015; NASA Earth Observatory 2015). That Indonesia's fires are burning not only forests but peat lands as well makes the situation more worrisome. Made up of dead and decaying plant material, peat lands are carbon-rich and also release methane, a GHG at least twenty times more potent than carbon.

This makes the impact of Indonesia's fires two hundred times greater than forest fires elsewhere. Peat land fires are also very difficult to extinguish and can smolder underground for months (Harris, Minnemeyer, Stolle, and Payne 2015).

Governance is a defining factor in forest management. In Indonesia, penalties for starting forest fires include jail terms of up to ten years, fines of up to ten million dollars, and closure of business operations. However, laws against forest fires are hardly enforced. Accountability is also extremely complex given the various actors involved (community, private business, government and nongovernment) across the various types of land (corporate concessions, state land, private, and communal lands). Indonesia would need to review its policy on peat lands, as peat lands less than nine feet deep are allowed to be cleared.

Within the Association of Southeast Asian Nations, a Transboundary Haze Pollution Agreement which seeks to mitigate haze pollution and control forest fires has been in force since 2003. Singapore in 2015 has begun legal proceedings against Indonesian companies allegedly behind the fires. The Agreement has yet to prove its effectiveness.

Evacuations continue and thousands continue to flee from affected provinces. However, as Zamzami found out, as fires continue and are expected to continue in 2016, evacuees may have nowhere to go.

Children play without wearing any protection at the playground while the air is engulfed with thick haze from the forest fires at Sei Ahass village, Kapuas district in Central Kalimantan province on Borneo island, Indonesia. These fires are a threat to the health of millions. Smoke from landscape fires kills an estimated 110,000 people every year across Southeast Asia, mostly as a result of heart and lung problems, and weakening newborn babies.

Photo credit: "Haze in Central Kalimantan" © Ardiles Rante/Greenpeace.

While REDD+ offers transformational change with its economic incentives, moving away from the usual business trajectory creates huge challenges. There will always be political and economic forces that benefit from deforestation and degradation. Effective implementation depends on good governance and reliable institutions. Reliable carbon monitoring is also required to support the results-based systems.

REDD+ offers different roles and responsibilities for countries and for the international community. Developing countries implementing REDD+ need financial and technical assistance from more developed countries. An investment of $30 billion a year in the REDD+ tropical forest conservation initiative can accelerate the global transition to green and sustainable growth. As of 2014, REDD+ is backed by $6.27 billion (UNEP International Resource Panel 2014).

Not all forests are the same. With their high biomass, tropical forests store on average about 50 percent more carbon than temperate forests per unit area (Porrura, Corbera, and Brown 2007). From the climate perspective, preserving forest cover and reforesting cleared areas in the tropics will more effectively slow temperature increases than planting trees across temperate croplands (Arora and Montenegro 2011). Among tropical forests, mangroves are among the most carbon-rich. Thus, despite accounting for just 0.7 percent of tropical forest area, mangrove deforestation contributes as much as 10 percent of GHG emissions from global deforestation (Donato et al. 2011).

A forest management strategy toward increasing forest carbon stocks, while producing a sustainable yield of timber, could keep forests growing at a higher rate over a longer period of time. Instead of allowing the natural decomposition or burning of wood, managed forests will delay the decay of wood from harvested wood products. Wood products with long life cycles will store carbon for years into the future, generating mitigation benefits.

Restoring degraded lands is another option. Niger, one of the world's poorest nations, offers a prime example of a land and tree tenure program to support regeneration of trees that benefited 4.5 million people, by increasing food production and farmers' incomes and creating new markets. Brazil and Indonesia seem to be recognizing that they have vast tracks of degraded forest lands with the potential for restoration and reuse in creating agricultural jobs without clearing more forests.

Afforestation and reforestation, while laudable, are not stand-alone programs with respect to climate change—these cannot offset increasing CO_2 emissions from deforestation and fossil fuel. Decreasing GHG emissions—whether from fossil fuels or land-use changes—is far more important. Forests should be kept as forests. While it is true that replanted forests can store the same amount of carbon, forests can take hundreds of years to grow.

Based on a 2013 study, reforestation of areas affected by land use would reduce atmospheric CO_2 by 40–70 ppm by the end of the century. This reduction is vastly dwarfed by continued global deforestation which is projected to increase CO_2 levels by 130–290 ppm by 2100. Fossil-fuel emissions are projected to increase CO_2 levels by 170–600 ppm by 2100 (Mackey et al. 2013).

Forest protection was found to be more effective when sustainable use by local populations was allowed rather than the total barring of protected areas. In Thailand and Costa Rica, local communities increased incomes with improved natural resources management. In Africa, Asia, and Latin America, protection programs in which indigenous peoples were included reduced deforestation rates by two percentage points a year (ECG 2010). This suggests that giving local people a stake in forest conservation can simultaneously address forest protection and economic development. The effectiveness of this approach depends on the ability and interest of communities to manage their forests—linked to their dependence on forest-based livelihoods. Tenure security is also necessary.

All forest efforts bank on coherent polices and consistent enforcement. Some attribute the decline in deforestation in the Brazilian Amazon to property rights and governance. In Indonesia, the burning of forests and peat lands continues despite laws against this practice, resulting in dangerous haze enveloping Southeast Asian cities every year.

Private companies also have immense influence on the state of global deforestation. Businesses independently committing to deforestation-free palm oil while protecting local communities will go a long way to preserving forests.

Urban Resilience and Mitigation

Globally, roughly 3.9 billion of the world's 7.2 billion people are urban. Acting as the world's growth centers—hosting production, trade, and financial hubs—cities create more than 80 percent of global GDP. As urban populations are projected to reach two-thirds of the world's population by 2050, the concentration of economic activities is expected to be more pronounced. These numbers underscore the relevance of urban centers in global interests and development concerns. Securing the world's cities is a primary interest.

Yet, a number of the world's largest cities are built on flood plains or low-lying coastal areas. At the same time, garbage, loss of mangroves, and loss of permeable surfaces common to urban areas compound the geographical risks. Some one billion people live in slums, heightening risks further.

The continued influx of migrants aggravates the situation as cities struggle to keep up with growth, often falling short. This is most true in middle-income countries in Africa and Asia, where populations are surging. Drastic increases in demand in transportation and housing are difficult to fill. And job opportunities often fall short of expectations. The Bangladeshi capital Dhaka, already home to fifteen million residents, still receives some 350,000 migrants annually. With this growth, its land-use planning and emergency service delivery cannot keep up. India, meanwhile, will have an additional four hundred million city dwellers by 2050. And in the developed world, demand for homes in the United Kingdom is pushing construction on to flood plains once considered too risky for built structures (Jack 2014).

However, the same dynamism that creates extreme demands from cities can also provide opportunity. With the convergence of human and capital resources, cities are in the best position to engineer a low-carbon path and build resilience. Astute leadership and effective governance are needed for this to come into play. Moreover, it is not enough to implement some solid waste policy or invest in some solar or flood control infrastructure. With the complexity of urban settings, a thorough, comprehensive, and workable plan in mitigation, adaptation, and DRR is needed.

City layout and climate-smart infrastructure are central to building protection against hazards of nature, and essential in accommodating future growth. These should be well thought out, especially since these will be very difficult to undo. Since most cities are located on high-risk flood plains or coastal areas, and abandoning them is out of the question, re-engineering and retrofitting cities may be part of the solution. Limiting new development on flood plains and coastal areas must be considered. The Netherlands, aside from building large-scale flood management infrastructure, has also resorted to floating homes and expansion of green spaces for water absorption.

A study of 136 coastal cities around the world has shown that coastlines as we know them will cease to exist if GHG emissions are not controlled. Exposure to floods in coastal cities continues to rise due to increasing populations, growth in assets, changing climate, and land subsidence. Average global flood losses will increase to $52 billion by 2050 (from $6 billion in 2005) due to socioeconomic changes alone. With climate change and land subsidence, flood loss estimate balloons to over a trillion US dollars per year if current flood protection investments remain at current levels and are not upgraded (Hallegatte et al. 2013).

Existing coastal defenses designed for current environmental conditions will be unable to withstand even modest increases in sea level. To reduce unacceptable losses, present protection will have to be strengthened. Coastal cities must manage the increase in risk before disaster hits. Major investments in coastal protection will be needed in the next decades. Disaster preparedness, reconstruction, and international collaboration, ultimately, are important, especially when small or poor countries are affected.

While they may have the most to gain in building resilience against climate change, cities also have a special responsibility. With their concentration of activities and people, cities account for more than 70 percent of global GHG emissions and are central to climate change mitigation strategies. Estimates show that GHG emissions could decrease by 10 percent annually if the world's hundred largest cities were to take the low-carbon route (World Bank 2014). The positive impact of cities shifting to a low-carbon path will resonate beyond cities' borders, but cities themselves may gain the most from such a move. It is interestingly fortunate that schemes to make cities greener and more efficient, and with the smallest carbon footprint, will also lead to healthier people, more resilient communities, and more inclusive development.

Globally, annual PM10 levels increased by 6 percent from 2009 to 2012.[4] Based on the World Health Organization's Ambient Air database,[5] Delhi is the most polluted city, followed by Karachi and Dakar (WHO 2014b). Pollution in India is not limited to Delhi. With over 70 percent of India's urban agglomerations failing air quality standards, it is not surprising that the country suffers the most deaths from chronic respiratory diseases. Reducing particulates through a low-carbon and cleaner growth path is estimated to prolong some 660 million Indian lives by over three years (Greenstone et al. 2015). In the People's Republic of China, aside from Beijing and Shanghai, which frequent the pollution headlines, cities north of the Huai River (in northern area) have been subjected to higher levels of total suspended particulates from coal for boilers for winter heating. This increased concentration of particulate shortens life expectancies of some five hundred million Chinese by 5.5 years (Chen et al. 2013).

As with adaptation and DRR, cities' actions toward climate change mitigation must begin with city plans and infrastructure. We look forward to more compact yet connected cities, with efficient buildings, and built around mass public transport. Low-carbon urban actions are estimated to generate savings to the amount of $16.6 trillion up to 2050. Urban mitigation actions can also reduce annual GHG emissions by 3.7 Gt CO_2 in 2030—14 percent of the 27 Gt CO_2 recommended reductions to limit warming by 2°C (Global Commission on the Economy and Climate 2015).

In transportation, aside from ensuring the resilience of transport infrastructure from floods and storms, cleaner and more energy-efficient modes of transportation must be in place. Shifting from roads to rails and the use of more energy efficient technologies must be prescribed. Liquid and gaseous biofuels are now commercially available, and low-carbon sources of electricity create the mitigation potential of electric rails and vehicles. Compact and well-planned cities may even limit the need for motorized transport, as well as reduce the need for travel.

Emissions from waste almost doubled from 1970 to 2010. And since waste generation is closely linked to population, affluence, and urbanization, efficient waste management is another mitigation action for cities. The main GHG from municipal solid waste disposal on land and from wastewater is methane, a gas more efficient in trapping heat than CO_2. Waste reduction, reuse, recycling, and energy recovery can significantly reduce emissions from waste disposal.

Driven by strong political will, the success of Curitiba's smart urban development strategy illustrates how environmentally sustainable urban development can be deliberately achieved at the subnational level (see box 4.3). While strong political leadership was key to this success, the cooperation and support of its residents also played a critical role in the Brazilian city's success.

Mitigation: Win-Win and Net-Win

Maintaining Asia's high growth remains a primary objective and is not to be put aside to make way for environmental aspirations. Yet, to

Box 4.3. Sustainable urban development: Curitiba, Brazil.

A key feature of Curitiba's urban development was to grow from the city core outward in a "radial-linear-branching pattern." Supported with an appropriate and energy-efficient public transport infrastructure, this diverted the traffic from the city center to the radial axes of housing, services, and industrial zones. Taking into account wind direction, the Curitiba Industrial City was established on the city's west side to avoid pollution in the urban center. Strict environmental regulations, including a ban on polluting industries, were implemented at the Curitiba Industrial City. The city also promoted waste-management infrastructure and public awareness of waste separation and recycling.

Despite population growth of over 3 percent per year, the average green area per person also increased from one square kilometer to over fifty from 1960 to 2008. Though one of the most affluent cities in Brazil, Curitiba has 25 percent lower per capita GHG emissions and 30 percent lower fuel consumption than the national average. Curitiba has the highest rate of public transport use (45 percent of journeys) in Brazil, and enjoys one of the country's lowest rates of urban air pollution. Per capita loss due to time spent in severe congestion in Curitiba is about eleven times less than in Sao Paulo and seven times less than in Rio de Janeiro.

With 70 percent of the city's residents actively recycling, 13 percent of solid waste is recycled in Curitiba, compared to only 1 percent in Sao Paulo. Curitiba Industrial City now accommodates over seven hundred companies and has created about fifty thousand direct jobs and 150,000 indirect jobs after three decades.

Curitiba has also managed to address its potentially costly flooding problems through a combination of flood control and drainage measures. Areas vulnerable to flooding were converted into parks and planted with many trees. Artificial lakes were also created to hold floodwaters. The cost of this strategy, including the relocation costs of slum dwellers, is estimated to be five times less than building concrete canals. As a result, property values of neighboring areas appreciated, and tax revenues increased.

Source: Global Commission on the Economy and Climate (2014).

protect the development gains logged through years of historically high economic growth, an environmentally sustainable path is necessary. These multiple goals will have to be pursued simultaneously. Propitiously, there are win-win, net-win, and synergistic policies that will advance both growth and environmental sustainability, and climate change mitigation in particular.

Ending energy subsidies is one win-win option that will generate positive environmental and economic results. Removing the regressive effects of subsidies, where the rich gain more, will help reduce inequality. Net-win policies, such as switching to a low-carbon path, may impose upfront economic costs in new investments and new technologies, but will also generate economic, social, and environmental benefits.

Most governments are still missing opportunities to pursue win-win strategies. A general neglect of rigorous monitoring and evaluation reinforces the negative view of efficiency-oriented projects as too demanding and ineffective. Timely, comprehensive, and consistent international monitoring of energy subsidies or prices is not in place, and basic national data on key factors related to energy efficiency are mostly lacking.

Timely and accurate data on household, commercial, municipal, industrial consumption, and expenditures on energy, are also in short supply. Without such basic data, opportunities for enhancing energy efficiency and improving inclusive access are difficult to identify and measure. This perpetuates the cycle of good intentions but missed opportunities in mitigation and productivity growth.

Given the variability in comparative advantage among countries, each must do what is necessary to become more resilient to the effects of a rise in temperatures, climate change, and natural disasters. For less affluent countries, in general, it pays to conserve natural capital and natural ecosystems more than it does to enforce complex incentives to scale up green technologies. But nothing is inherently wrong with pursuing innovative and inexpensive, high-tech and low-carbon solutions tailored specifically for poor countries. This book advocates that each country build its own boat, without waiting for a consensus on the details of the international environmental blueprints.

Notes

1. High emitting industries have high average emissions, high emissions intensity, and account for 89 percent of corporate emissions reported to Carbon Disclosure Program; and include energy, utilities, materials (chemical, metals, and mining), and industrials (airlines, air freight, and marine).
2. Australia, Denmark, Finland, France, Germany, Italy, Japan, the Netherlands, Sweden, the United Kingdom, and the United States.
3. Energy service companies provide and install energy efficiency equipment and building refurbishment to final energy users to save energy.
4. PM10: Fine particulate matter of ten microns or less
5. Database of sixteen hundred cities from 91 countries.

5

Climate Adaptation and Disaster Management

We cannot avoid natural hazards, but we know enough,
to certainly, prevent them to become disasters.
—Margareta Wahlström, Special Representative of the
UN Secretary-General for Disaster Risk Reduction

With at least $40 billion a year needed for climate adaptation in Asia and the Pacific, climate adaptation can no longer be left to gradual and ad hoc measures. Failure to make it a development priority could slow the pace of economic growth and social progress in the years ahead. Disaster losses are not inevitable and can be reduced through collaborative action.

While managing disasters has always been a concern, climate change has raised the stakes. DRR involves understanding exposure and hazard sensitivity, and the location-specific connections between climate change, natural disasters, and other risks. The predictability of some disasters makes the case for disaster planning much more compelling. DRR is becoming a key part of the needed strategy. And while this book focuses on climate-related disasters, this chapter will include lessons from how people prepare for and respond to earthquakes and tsunamis that can be applied to disasters in general.

People living along cyclone tracks, in coastal areas, and in floodplains expect the yearly storms and floods. Hazard maps must therefore guide community planning and zoning laws. And limiting populations exposed in these areas is one clear measure of risk reduction.

In Rio, Argentina, job opportunities attracted some sixty thousand people to build houses on the steep hillsides right above the city. In January 2010, 740 people died and over twenty-one thousand people were made homeless when a massive flood hit the area. The enforcement of land zoning proved to be inadequate. In Brazil, the absence of urban planning has been blamed for cities' vulnerability to floods. In 2010 and 2011, flash floods and landslides destroyed hillside neighborhoods and claimed the lives of over a thousand people. Since land in city centers are too expensive, settlements continue to thrive on high-risk mountain slopes and hillsides.

During 1991–2010, global disaster losses reached $862.0 billion (Kellet and Caravani 2013). In the same period, $106.7 billion (or 3.6 percent) of the $3 trillion in official development assistance worldwide was allocated to disasters. Of the $106.7 billion official development assistance for disasters, $69.9 billion went into emergency response, $23.3 billion for reconstruction and rehabilitation, and $13.5 billion for disaster preparedness and prevention. For every $100 of official development assistance, only forty cents go into DRR.

DRR is not the sole responsibility of governments and humanitarian and emergency agencies. It also concerns communities and individuals. It is a responsibility of all, for no one is immune to disaster impacts. Margareta Wahlström, UN's special representative of the secretary-general for DRR and head of UNISDR, has argued that businesses need to see disasters as a risk to themselves, and is therefore a core business interest.

Strengthening the capacity of people, lifelines, and infrastructure to withstand and rapidly recover from a hazard will limit losses and disruptions—and can even prevent hazards from turning into disasters. Building disaster resilience, especially in countries highly vulnerable to the effects of climate change, should be considered a priority.

Box 5.1. Good practices in resilience, adaptation, and disaster risk reduction.

While there are no hard-and-fast rules, these cases demonstrate the following principles for building resilience and effective disaster management.

- Investments in the hard and soft components of resilience are equally important. Resilient infrastructure and engineering must be complemented by education, knowledge, and training.
- Collaboration and coordination among various players will maximize impact, but local community involvement is key.
- Strategies must be informed by all useful knowledge and technology—modern and scientific, as well as local and indigenous experience.

Case 1. Sendai City, Japan, is located on the Pacific side of the Tohoku region. Sendai City is vulnerable to frequent earthquakes and flooding during the rainy season.

After the 1995 Great Hanshin/Awaji Earthquake, Sendai provided subsidies for the seismic retrofitting of detached wooden houses, the removal of concrete-brick walls, and putting in hedges. The city has also retrofitted hospital and schools. Sendai schools have established a school disaster response system and conducts evacuation training twice a year. The importance of training was confirmed during the Great East Japan Earthquake. In the three schools located along the coast that were hit by the tsunami, no children on school grounds died in the disaster.

Sendai has comprehensive flood control measures in place with storm drains and a city sewerage system that can handle once-in-a-decade torrential rains.

Case 2. Community-based disaster preparedness in Indian Ocean countries.

In the aftermath of the 2004 Indian Ocean tsunami, UNISDR was tasked to develop a tsunami early warning system across the twenty-eight countries of the Indian Ocean region. Emphasizing risk education, monitoring and warning services, communication, and preparedness and response capability, the project has generated its share of success stories.

Signboards along Sri Lanka's coast direct residents to safer ground.

Photo credit: From www.irinnews.org, by Amantha Perera/IRIN, © 2010 United Nations. Reprinted with the permission of the United Nations.

In Sri Lanka, flood and landslide monitoring systems and early warning dissemination mechanisms were already in place by the time the floods and landslides struck in 2007. Armed with hazard maps and the forecast using GPS instruments, evacuations were effectively implemented putting populations out of danger. In the Nuwara Eliya District, fifty-six families were evacuated in time and resulted in no casualties. Aside from access to risk and hazard information, the key to the successful evacuation was the development of response capabilities: disaster awareness sessions, training of local authorities, and setting up of standard operating procedures for communities.

Case 3. Indigenous Knowledge for DRR: Singas Village of Papua New Guinea and the Ivatans of the Philippines.

Singas village is situated in Morobe Province along the banks of a major river in Papua New Guinea. The river, which is the major source of livelihood for the village, also brings about yearly flooding. Rejecting the call to leave the river bank, villagers instead resort to indigenous knowledge to reduce the impact of floods. Settlements are on high ground and away from lava flow. Using traditional and accessible bush materials, villagers build their houses on stilts with large mounds under to stem the rising flood water. Traditional bush materials are cheap, transportable and easy to manage. The Singas village also has a comprehensive drainage system dug out by hand. While gardens are planted along the river bank to take advantage of the fertile soil, planting season avoids the rainy season to minimize disruption.

Singas houses on stilts (left) and Ivatan traditional house (right)

Photo credit: From Indigenous Knowledge for Disaster Risk Reduction: Good Practices and Lessons Learned from Experiences in the Asia-Pacific Region, © 2008 United Nations. Reprinted with the permission of the United Nations.

The Ivatans of the Philippines' northernmost province of Batanes have also learned to adapt to typhoons and rough seas. While houses of bamboo with nipa palm roofs are customary for the rest of the country, Ivatans have learned to build houses that can withstand typhoons and strong winds. Built with limestone walls two to four feet thick, and layers upon layers of reeds and cogon grass as roofing, these structures are clustered to protect one another. Composed of a cluster of islands, fishing and boat making are traditional activities. Ivatans' traditional wooden boats have rounded bottoms that roll with the waves.

Sources: http://www.unisdr.org/campaign/resilientcities/cities/view/1065, UNISDR (2008), and UNISDR (2010).

Disaster Management Cycle

To soften the impact of hazards, lessons from previous events must inform courses of action, which must encompass all stages of disaster management. Disaster management cycles can be divided into equally important phases: pre-disaster, disaster relief, and reconstruction and recovery (figure 5.1). Much more must be done to prepare for disasters, before disaster strikes, rather than reacting only after the fact. Although the precise location, timing, or intensity of a hazard is unpredictable, disasters tend to concentrate and recur in certain regions or countries. For this reason, a variety of measures can be taken before a disaster strikes.

No one country typifies good practices, but there are examples to build on. Capacity to respond is extremely vital, as shown by the experiences of Malaysia and Singapore in search and rescue. Thailand, in the wake of the 2011 floods, promoted catastrophe insurance for small businesses.

Bangladesh's cyclone warning system is another good example. After Cyclone Bhola, with wind speeds of two hundred kilometers per hour, killed over five hundred thousand people in 1970, Bangladesh invested $10 billion on cyclone readiness. With the country equipped with early warning systems, disaster-resilient shelters, and embankment

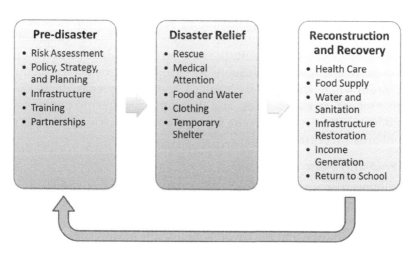

Figure 5.1. Disaster management cycle.

Source: Author's illustration adapted from Strauss (n.d.) and Todd and Todd (2011).

protection, Cyclone Sidr in 2007, with wind speeds of 250 kilometers per hour, led to a much lower death toll at ten thousand (Thorlund and Potutan 2015).

It is important to mobilize funds, secure investments for DRR, and build capacities across institutions for disaster monitoring and response before disaster strikes. When it does strike, mobilizing the necessary proactive and immediate response then requires building on institutional and financial capacities from the earlier stage (Todd and Todd 2011).

Actions in each phase have implications for the management and effectiveness of the subsequent phase, and each deserves equal attention. Undervaluing DRR, for instance, leads to a culture where rehabilitation and reconstruction prevail disproportionately. Disaster management becomes lop-sided, as in many disaster-prone countries. Some flood programs in Pakistan focused heavily on rebuilding infra-structure. Investments that would better protect the population such as early warning systems and flood control measures were neglected. The impulse to satisfy urgent needs by replacing what was lost often outweigh the desire to build back better, which would take longer.

While every disaster is unique, there will always be lessons to be learned from past experiences. Past disasters and disaster relief operations can still inform us as to what works and what doesn't in managing and reducing disaster risk. Nonetheless, lessons from past disasters need to be assessed carefully for their appropriateness or relevance to specific situations. Developing formal disaster prepared-ness models can be difficult, because recommendations based on comparative empirical evaluations are virtually nonexistent. Providing a forum where stakeholders involved in disaster preparedness can interact, share experiences, and develop a disaster preparedness model together is perhaps the best method of general applicability and broad acceptance.

Pre-disaster Phase

Building preparedness is less visible than the disaster response or post-disaster phases, but it is equally important. Developing capa-bilities, preparedness, and resilience takes time, and is almost always underemphasized, but the payoff is almost always very high.

Countries subject to recurring hazards should incorporate pre-paredness and preventive measures, as well as response strategies in development plans. Funding and support for national institutions and local governments to provide the necessary infrastructure and know-how must be well placed. The outpouring of solidarity and support that usually arise in the aftermath of disasters must also be present in prevention and pre-disaster activities.

That prevention and pre-disaster actions save lives must be broadcast. Early warning systems and preemptive evacuation have saved lives. The whole population of Tulang Diyot—a tiny island off the mainland in Cebu, Philippines—was saved from the wrath of Typhoon Haiyan when preemptive evacuation was enforced. While not one house was left after the Typhoon, all one thousand inhabitants were saved (McElroy 2013). In India, the evacuation of more than a million people before Cyclone Phailin is credited with saving thousands of lives. Key factors in the successful evacuation were improved forecasting services and early warning systems. Warnings and alerts which used various channels—news networks, mobile phone text messages, satellite phones, and loudspeakers—were disseminated as early as four days before the cyclone struck. Cyclone shelters provided safety to more than one hundred thousand people.

Aside from early warning systems, resilient and accessible infrastructure for safe water, hospitals, and evacuation centers are among the most important investments. From Asia to Latin America, breaks in these lifelines are major causes of desperation and breakdown in order that often follows climate-related disasters and earthquakes. Facilities vital to crisis response must be linked to networks that will not fail them. So when the earth shakes or when the waters rise, critical networks can stay disaster-resilient and victims need not turn on each other to survive.

Seismic retrofitting of hospitals in Sendai, Japan enabled people to continue functioning after the 2011 Tohoku earthquake. In contrast, emergency medical facilities in Chile, Haiti, and the Philippines dropped off-line just when they were needed the most. Many more lives may have been saved and recovery would have been much easier had connectivity to emergency medical care and water remained in place.

Disaster-proofing hospitals, by one measure, adds less than a tenth to the cost of new hospitals, while rebuilding a destroyed hospital virtually doubles its initial cost. These systems also need to be assured of uninterrupted power supply, a network of protected access routes, and a secure provision of safe water and sanitation. In too many countries, facilities that are critical for an effective response are tied to networks that are almost guaranteed to fail.

The failure of infrastructure would routinely interrupt vital services, leading to power failures, water supply disruption, and mobility restrictions. Damaged roads and fallen bridges consistently limit people's movement to safer areas, in addition to shackling the delivery of life-saving medicines and hospital supplies.

Hazards of nature pose systematic risks to development, especially in highly populated urban areas. Low-lying coastal megacities in Asia especially need a climate adaptation and disaster resilience strategy. Flooding can be reduced significantly by cleaning and expanding drainage systems and improving pumping capacities. Climate proofing infrastructure and building lifelines may be especially difficult in poorly governed Asian cities, with sprawling settlements developed over marshlands and natural catch basins, complex labyrinths of overburdened storm drains, disaster-prone natural topographies, and a stock of structurally insecure old buildings and infrastructure.

Disaster Relief

The principal concern of the initial disaster response is saving lives and providing basic needs—water, food, shelter, clothing, and medical assistance. The ability or inability to provide immediate critical care also has a cascading impact on the whole recovery process. Medium-term response is directly involved in recovery, starting with damage assessments. Intermediate measures will be taken to restore the structures and functions of communities and institution.

Important characteristics that effectively support disaster response include speed, timeliness, inclusion, transparency, and flexibility. Rapid and timely response helps limit casualties and damage to property and livelihoods. Inclusion and transparency promote ownership and social cohesion that are also essential for effective response. And the orderly distribution of emergency supplies involving local leadership is important in maintaining social cohesion. Flexibility, especially in the design of activities and procurement procedures, is also critical for the effectiveness and efficiency of disaster response. Incorporating all these characteristics at the same time may prove difficult enough to necessitate prioritizing and establishing trade-offs between the equally desirable program characteristics. This should be made in the context of the entire disaster management cycle.

After 2004's Hurricane Ivan in Grenada and Santa Lucia, families that did not lose their dwellings took in friends and relatives. A recognition of this normal human tendency helped governments scale down their shelter programs. This had an unexpected symbiotic effect: not only did such actions provide immediate relief to those who had lost their homes, they also helped preserve existing social relationships to the advantage of the community.

All disaster response activities, especially those providing urgent and critical interventions, are ultimately the responsibility of national governments. However, the involvement of a broad range of stakeholders will always be crucial. A government may be so weakened by disasters that it may compromise its ability to provide, control, and coordinate immediate relief and response. Engagement of a broad range of stakeholders will help bridge the gaps and help ensure that response covers the basic emergency needs across all sectors of the communities affected. This will also encourage broad-based support.

A reasonable amount of streamlining is required to come up with a coordinated and effective disaster response among the various players—government, local, and international organizations, and foreign governments. Immediately after the 2005 Pakistani earthquake, hundreds of aid groups and foreign workers poured in to help. To avoid a scenario in which some areas receive a surplus of aid while others are never reached, a group of economists set up an office where aid information could be gathered. Unfortunately, most agencies refused to cooperate (Banerjee 2006).

Reconstruction and Recovery

Immediately after the emergency stage, a necessary first step in recovery and reconstruction is the rapid assessment of the magnitude of the disaster's damage to life, property, crops, livelihoods, infrastructure, and institutions. This should be quick, well-coordinated, detailed, and focused to guide immediate planning of post-disaster recovery and reconstruction. The assessment should also be continually updated as the situation unfolds.

During the post-disaster response, it is crucial to restore disrupted social relationships. Creating trust among victims of a shared disaster is relatively easy and can make recovery smoother, more efficient, and sustainable.

Gender-sensitive interventions are often forgotten in the rush to act in post-disaster situations, worsening social relationships that may already be fragile. Simple sensitivities can help. Layout of temporary shelters and design of public places should give special attention to the needs of women. Ensuring that doors face well-lit areas, avoiding dark alleys and passages, can help reduce crimes against women. Women have been found to be more resilient than men in traumatic situations, and ensuring their safety will make post-disaster responses even more sustainable.

A number of post-disaster actions can effectively reduce collective suffering, restore livelihoods, and help people get back on their feet and recover. After the 2005 earthquake in Pakistan, many feared that more people would starve or freeze to death as winter hit the remote mountainous region. Cash transfers and emergency shelters provided by the Government of Pakistan, with the support of United Nations (UN) and donor countries, proved especially helpful, and prevented another catastrophe.

Restoring communities to their original physical state may not be sufficient. Physical risks and social and economic vulnerabilities are why disasters frequently hit and affect the same people or areas. In the recovery and reconstruction phase, these risks and vulnerabilities must be reduced to help avert future disasters. Relocation and building better will help decrease exposure and vulnerabilities. Food and cash for work programs are short-term measures often used during and after disasters. Long-term initiatives can have a greater impact. Skill building and vocational programs to increase employability after the recovery period can be crucial. Even more broadly, governments should link their national food security plans with disaster preparedness and response in hazardous regions.

Program and Project Design. Program and project designs should be based on local cultures and capacities and the realities of post-disaster situations. Design of disaster recovery and reconstruction projects should account for the diminished government capacity which is typical after a disaster.

As a case in point, the Sri Lanka Tsunami Emergency Recovery Program was processed rapidly under the World Bank's emergency guidelines. Though its targets were largely achieved, government resources were stretched to the limit. Involvement of nongovernment organizations and UN agencies can fill gaps and improve performance and capacity, but their participation should not foster dependency (Todd and Todd 2011).

Emergency projects require special attention to the design and implementation of disbursement arrangements. To ensure a smooth cash flow, clear implementation and disbursement guidelines and regulations must all be in order. Technical assistance to first-time borrowers and training in procurement procedures must also be provided.

Simplicity in project design makes for effective implementation. Disaster response projects should limit the number of implementing agencies and sectors involved. Implementation should be flexible to ensure responsiveness to community needs and external conditions that may change rapidly and unexpectedly.

Piggybacking on existing activities is especially advantageous in governing post-disaster instruments such as social funds—whose institutionalized operational procedures provide an immediate implementation platform to reach stakeholders who may be overlooked otherwise.

There is no perfect model for the messy and tragic situations after disasters. And because domestic governments are ultimately responsible, they need to experiment and, periodically, quickly evaluate feedback as part of their standard operating procedures. This will speed up disaster response and fine tune project design as the context unfolds.

Relocation and Reconstruction. It is critical to look out constantly for human actions or inactions that can, if not taken into account, turn recurring natural hazards into recurring natural disasters. Immediate steps need to feed into longer-term solutions. In responding urgently to reconstruction needs, a crucial lesson is to recover with care and promote disaster resilience by rebuilding in ways that improve on past practices and reduce the chance of recurrence. For instance, rebuilding substandard homes in disaster-prone areas may provide housing to people in need, but can lead to more severe losses if disaster strikes again. And this is most likely if aid, relocation plans, and reconstruction efforts are delayed.

Rebuilding better in the same spot versus relocating to a safer site often presents a dilemma. After a disaster, there is an insistent pressure to relocate communities on the one side, and to stay for reasons of tradition and livelihood on the other. This trade-off needs to be managed. The benefits and costs of relocation versus rebuilding better in situ need to be compared. The ability to enforce strict hazard zoning as well as to implement relocation plans can be challenging. Strong political will is required. Effective relocation involves the provision of adequate services and livelihood support to ensure that people will not go back to previously occupied, high-risk areas.

In the wake of Typhoon Haiyan, which left over four million people homeless in an area where most do not own land, relocation has been the byword. It is imperative that the government and the development community emphasize sustainability through community consultations (OXFAM 2014). Though homelessness is an urgent issue, resources may just be wasted if the new housing and relocation sites are abandoned. Apart from the physical housing structures, livelihoods and services must be provided. It is important that those affected do not fall deeper into poverty.

In most cases, the advantages of minimizing socioeconomic dislocation and building on existing infrastructure and community facilities are obvious. The familiarity with locations and old social networks can also boost resilience against future disasters better than the relative anonymity of a new location.

In many country situations, simpler measures can suffice. Raising houses above flood levels—by putting them on pillars or using higher foundations, can enhance the resilience of residents and structures. In Bangladesh, a post-flood housing reconstruction project introduced capping of traditional earth plinths with cement-stabilized soil. This proved very effective in subsequent floods. Other examples of disaster-resilient housing built after a disaster follow similar principles, often by reinforcing existing structures with materials and techniques involving higher structural standards.

Still on Bangladesh, improving access to hygienic water and sanitation facilities helped communities cope with recurrent disasters. Providing elevated tube-wells and flood-proof latrines ensured year-round safe water and hygienic sanitation in flood-prone districts. Where impounding reservoirs existed, as in the Khulna district, increasing their size or relocating the water-intake point further upstream boosted the resilience of water supply systems (ADB 2011).

After the 1984 earthquake in Armenia, temporary shelters were built using construction techniques that improved disaster resistance. Following the 2005 earthquake in Kashmir, Pakistan, the Rural Housing Reconstruction Program rehabilitated and reconstructed houses to seismic-resistant standards, trained local masons and foremen, and strengthened logistics for the provision of quality materials. These have made housing safer to face future hazards.

Eight months after Hurricane Sandy, the government of New York City launched its plan to climate-proof major parts of the city, not only to improve its disaster resilience, but also to increase investor confidence. A new, flood-proof neighborhood called Seaport City is expected to rise from the East River in lower Manhattan, and Staten Island is to see twenty-foot flood walls along its southern shore with levees envisioned to flank coastal neighborhoods in all five boroughs. Constructed above a flood protection system, the plan, which includes addition of wetlands and tidal barriers, would make many subway and utility structures resilient to flooding (Fermino 2013).

Quick initial recovery actions based on the rapid assessments and realistic schedules for reconstruction projects help minimize losses and contribute to post-disaster success. A phased reconstruction program, where the sequencing of activities is prioritized carefully, will deliver better outcomes. And although highly undesirable in urgent relief activities, staggered disbursement of aid funds may actually reduce inflationary pressures and leakage.

To promote the reconstruction of houses, it is important to involve homeowners. This approach succeeded in two major projects in India and one in Turkey where homeowners were assisted in managing the reconstruction of their own homes, rather than engaging general contractors (World Bank 2003a, 2007b, 2009a). Homeowners were provided with access to conditional funds for housing repair. The process improved enforcement of safety guidelines and minimized costs of arbitrary and unnecessary follow-up.

The involvement of the community also proved very effective in Nepal's School Earthquake Safety Program when a simple school retrofit evolved into a comprehensive program of earthquake safety. When builders received on-the-job training in earthquake-resistant design, they were also convinced of the benefits and affordability of earthquake-resistant buildings (Asian Disaster Preparedness Center 2003). This had important multiplier effects, as the builders then convinced homeowners to construct earthquake-resistant houses.

Investments in infrastructure are compromised by the failure to fund and carry out maintenance. Governments in developing countries tend to borrow to rebuild, but often make inadequate provision for maintenance, which is essential for long-term sustainability. Budget constraints and a lack of maintenance culture within institutions partly explain this. The Flood Damage Restoration Project in Pakistan demonstrated that adequate maintenance and sound asset management that reduce risks from subsequent disasters should complement restoration of facilities. Poorly maintained facilities increase vulnerability. Adequate maintenance is crucial for schools and other community facilities that double as evacuation centers during natural disasters. Maintenance funding for infrastructure could be increased by raising budget appropriations for this purpose, by setting aside a portion of development aid for maintenance purposes or, where appropriate, by drawing on user fees, tariffs, and other mechanisms as preventive expenditures.

Social Safety Nets

Social safety nets are transfer programs seeking to prevent the poor or the most vulnerable from falling below a certain level of poverty. In reducing disaster risk, highly vulnerable groups, such as the very young and old, the disabled, and ethnic minorities, need special consideration.

After the 2005 earthquake in Kashmir, the failure of authorities to provide housing and livelihood assistance to the most vulnerable and the most exposed was a major reason for long-term population displacement and protracted existence of temporary shelter settlements (IFRC 2005).

Explicit recognition of gender-related issues in natural disasters is also essential. In major disasters in Asia and the Pacific, the death toll for women is often substantially more than for men, because women have less control over key survival and recovery resources, including shelter and transport. Women comprised 91 percent of Cyclone Gorky victims in Bangladesh in 1991 and 67 percent of tsunami victims in Banda Aceh, Indonesia, in 2004. School children and youth are also more vulnerable to disaster when their schools have not been built to resist natural hazards. Public schools are often built on less valuable land, susceptible to flooding, earthquakes, or landslides. This helps explain why ten thousand schools collapsed during the 2005 Kashmir earthquake, killing seventeen thousand students and seriously injuring fifty thousand (ADB 2010).

Since social safety nets in developing countries are linked inextricably with issues of land ownership, an established and justified land-ownership system will help reduce vulnerability. In rural areas, the inability of many disaster victims to produce legal evidence of ownership jeopardizes disaster-related compensation. In such cases, feudal lords and big farmers with collateral power can capture disaster loans, depriving poor tenants and small farmers of what may be rightfully theirs. With safety nets compromised, their only source of funds to rehabilitate themselves are private money lenders and traditional landlords, who may be more than happy to extend loans and perpetuate dependency in normal and disaster situations. This practice needs to be recognized in post-disaster efforts among unequals affected by a common disaster (Prasad 1976).

Post-disaster operations therefore need to deal early and sternly with land-ownership issues, especially in informal urban settlements and rural areas. Where possible, land titles should be regularized or a functional proxy for land titles should be provided (as in the case of the Gujarat earthquake). In Banda Aceh, three-quarters of the land affected by the 2004 tsunami were not registered (Llyod-Jones 2006). Community land mapping activities are facilitating land title issues. Where such measures are not possible, alternatives need to be found to ensure that land-grabbing does not occur or that fraudulent claims are not honored. Local governments must control profiteering on land needed urgently for reconstruction purposes.

When floods destroyed houses along the Indus River basin in Pakistan, most victims migrated to cities. They preferred the stability of working as urban wage laborers rather than relying on the exploitative mercies of rural landlords. Under those conditions, disaster reconstruction must ensure that funds are not spent excessively on the better-off, who stay in disaster-struck areas and can manage without social safety nets.

Rebuilding or strengthening social safety nets for disaster victims should not be based on impulsive considerations or ad hoc compassion. They should be designed with an eye on how governments can fold such provisions into a wider welfare policy. The lesson holds true for post-disaster activities in general.

Governance

Good governance indicates a well-structured, integrated, and rational strategy in DRR and management, and adaptation. It also includes implementation: efficient and well-coordinated actions in the whole spectrum of actions from preemptive evacuations, disaster response, to relocations and reconstructions. There should be zero tolerance for corruption. In developing countries, corrupt practices, and not the lack of engineering capacity, are often the main constraint to building resilient infrastructure.

Local government plans must be integrated with national plans, and local policies coherent with national policies. Coordination between national and local units must be laid-out well for the smooth flow of work between different expertise, sectors, and community stakeholders.

Past disaster risk management projects in Bangladesh have had limited success as they have failed to develop links and collaboration between technical experts and policy makers, and among various offices (GFDRR n.d.).

Local governance and planning must recognize the role of communities, civil society, and the private sector. These sectors must be well-informed and educated on the resilience and development objectives of cities for them to participate and invest toward a unified goal. However, a balance must be achieved between a decentralized and a completely top-down governing process. Without sacrificing the participation of all stakeholders, effective governance must avoid delays and political stalemates between the various actors (Tanner et al. 2009).

Institutions

Steps are needed to professionalize the entire chain of institutions, processes, and individuals involved in DRR. Enabling institutional frameworks and sustained commitment are pivotal to enhancing resilience. Institutional frameworks—policy, legal, and regulatory—and sustained commitment are essential to ensure direction, coordination, and accountability in resilience efforts.

The Indian State of Maharashtra totally revamped its disaster risk management policies after the devastating Latur earthquake in 1993. Drawing on both international and local expertise, building standards and administrative legislation were improved (UNISDR 2004). Various Indian state governments have revised disaster policies and adopted more comprehensive disaster risk management in keeping with good governance practices. Whether or not those practices are enforced when they should be is another matter.

Building and supporting the capacity of existing institutions for reconstruction can often be a better option than creating new institutions.

Sri Lanka's reconstruction experience after the 2004 tsunami—the biggest natural disaster to ever hit the country—is a good example. A major bottleneck encountered during reconstruction was the lack of capacity in newly created central institutions, specifically the Task Force to Rebuild the Nation and the Reconstruction and Development Agency, and the lack of capacity in public procurement and in managing the large amounts of funding from donors (World Bank 2009b). The Task Force to Rebuild the Nation faced serious implementation challenges because of lack of capacity in procurement, public financial management, and coordination. The Reconstruction and Development Agency, which replaced the Task Force to Rebuild the Nation, encountered the same implementation issues.

To overcome problems associated with old versus new institutions, some observers stress continuity anchored in a professional cadre involved in disaster management (Haddow and Bullock 2003). Pakistan had greater success in mobilizing reconstruction efforts through the Earthquake Reconstruction and Rehabilitation Authority created after the 2005 earthquake. The agency developed its manpower from existing government resources. Experts were also critically selected and hired through donor assistance. With this set-up, the agency enjoyed the confidence of donors and other line agencies of the government.

Continuity and innovation coexist in useful ways in a disaster situation that needs established support systems and entrepreneurial action at the same time. Hybrid arrangements involving existing and new institutions need to pay close attention to agreeing on incremental staffing and workload increases before disaster reconstruction programs are scaled up.

Local Ownership and Partnerships

Effective governance needs to engage local governments and communities. Local governments have a better grasp of the local situation. And local stakeholders will be the ones directly involved and affected by actions.

Rapid development and processing of disaster-related interventions can present challenges of ownership. This can happen when several donors and partners attempt to begin their assistance programs at the earliest opportunity and sidestep local government structures. Bypassing institutions that are locally accountable allows powerful local stakeholders to control the process for their own benefit (DRLA 2011). Sidestepping local governments also reduces the confidence and capacity of local communities to represent themselves.

In the Samoa Cyclone Emergency Recovery Project, central government ministries made community grants easily accessible. Technical assistance was provided and communities were encouraged to take ownership of the resulting assets. This close involvement of the communities ensured that developed assets remained in good shape and were used even after the recovery project closed. In contrast, the Sri Lanka Tsunami Emergency Recovery Program's housing component was contractor-driven and did not encourage social mobilization. The program's inability to mobilize the community for a common purpose hindered follow-up in the post-disaster phase (Todd and Todd 2011).

In the aftermath of the Haiti earthquake, the sudden proliferation of large international organizations undermined local capacity and created unnecessary dependency. Twelve months after the devastating 2010 earthquake, more than one million Haitians remained in camps and substantive recovery had not begun (DRLA 2011). Similar issues were encountered in the aftermath of the 2004 tsunami. The sizeable international presence in Aceh, Indonesia, and Sri Lanka swamped local capacity. As a consequence, local and community-based organizations were poorly represented in consultations and coordination meetings (Bennett et al. 2006).

Beyond victims and existing community groups, effective governance needs to engage local nongovernment organizations that are usually the best suited to articulate the collective voice of the most exposed and the vulnerable. Engagement with locally based, credible, and competent nongovernment organizations can be important in minimizing the transaction costs of providing services and assisting disaster victims. Trust and familiarity can bypass the need to establish complex bureaucratic systems in disaster situations, allowing local entities to reach beneficiaries in timely and direct ways.

Government effectiveness in disaster response can be strengthened by leveraging existing private sector capacity, especially in areas such as infrastructure, structural improvements, and local banking. Similarly, working with existing international institutions that do not need screening for reputational risks and delivery capacity can improve response. International involvement must not ignore local roles and involvement.

Effective action requires strong partnerships. This the-more-the-better strategy implies cooperation among governments, development partners, the private sector, civil society, and local communities. But here, exceptional coordination becomes a necessity. The political economy can present risks or opportunities, and certain players will use their position to strengthen their own political or narrow economic interests. While well-entrenched political players are crucial to gaining broad commitment to action, their influence may not be permanent. Demands for risk reduction, prevention, and greater resilience are reinforced when coalitions of academic institutions, scientific bodies, the media, and advocacy organizations push strongly for them.

Disaster response projects or activities need to be developed and implemented rapidly. Reaching agreements with the government on risk reduction, prevention, and adaptation measures within the first three months is crucial because politicians tend to lose focus once the memory of disasters and emergency recedes. Once agreements are reached, they need to be locked into some form of public commitment, including consensus on financing mechanisms that can be used to keep governments accountable and on track.

Planning and implementation in post-disaster situations must follow the principle of blending participatory practices at the local level, with a more top-down approach in coordination and enforcement at a higher level. This abstract dictum requires cultivating sensitivity toward local and deeper contextual issues. When institutionalized successfully, this simple idea can have major implications for governance in disaster situations.

Information Technology

Better use of information and data management systems, grounded in a coherent institutional structure, presents opportunities to improve solutions in almost all aspects of disaster preparedness and response.

Collected data will be of most use if analyzed and shared on time for effective response. Local communities, governments, and organizations must be well-coordinated and provided with the information each needs. From the collection of data to its dissemination, and throughout the creation of links and coordination, the choice and use of technology must be suited to the local context.

Globally, there are very few who have developed and employed well-functioning information systems for disaster response. Financing is often the obstacle. Reallocating emergency funds for technological purposes can be difficult. Funds are neither available quickly nor offered for the long periods of time needed to develop, implement, and sustain technological platforms and systems.

The use of information technology has seen few successes at the local level. In the aftermath of the 2004 tsunami, use of mobile phones and satellite imagery in emergency response communications and coordination proved very helpful (Bennett et al. 2006). In 2013, thousands of lives in the Philippines were saved from Typhoon Bopha through early warnings and safety information sent to mobile phones (IFRC 2013b).

Communicating timely weather forecasts and hazard information to communities through mobile phones could save lives. Since much of this technology is in the hands of the private sector, partnerships between different sectors, including international stakeholders, must be improved.

The success of the cyclone warning system in Bangladesh proves that disaster preparedness is also good economics. Investing and developing early warning systems have saved countless lives and significantly reduced losses. It is also a good example of how information technology can strengthen institutional capacity in DRR and save lives.

6

Transforming Mindsets, Motivations, and Politics

The international community has not acted enough.
—Pope Francis

The greatest challenge in the fight against climate change is to show how switching to green growth is really more profitable than business as usual. Including carbon costs, ecosystem services, and disaster risks in policy and decision-making will demonstrate the benefits of green growth. The task is also to motivate individuals to change their mindsets to value future benefits as superior to gains rationalized by old convictions. After years of experience with mitigation and international agreements, a consensus seems to have emerged in principle: that the rising frequency and intensity of natural disasters and climate change are expressions of market and government failures; and solutions to change institutional practices and individual motivations must incorporate political economy constraints.

A big constraint in pursuing this understanding is due to policy makers and political leaders who also create or perpetuate problems associated with climate change and natural disasters. The majority of countries have continued to muddle through half-hearted attempts to tame the silent dangers of climate change and the fury of natural disasters. Very few countries—Germany, the Republic of Korea, the United Kingdom—have acted unilaterally and risen above self-interest to impose energy targets and feed-in tariffs. To make the structural transformation that the global economy needs, governments need to take a more active role (Stiglitz 2013).

Box 6.1 demonstrates how Germany decoupled GHG emissions from economic growth. Technology can be imported. With wind and solar increasingly becoming cost-competitive, other countries may find it cheaper to invest in energy efficiency and renewable technology. For countries with more sunshine than Germany, solar energy will be much cheaper, by producing more (as much as twice) power from the same solar panels.

Bridging the Knowledge Gap

Acting on climate change must be seen as good for growth and employment, as it offers benefits beyond its effect on disasters. Besides reducing carbon emissions, it can create green jobs.

Box 6.1. Germany decouples GHG emissions from economic growth.

In 1997, developed countries committed to reduce GHG emissions under the Kyoto Protocol. The European Union pledged an 8 percent reduction in the period 2008–2012 from 1990 levels. Germany for its part committed to a comparable 21 percent reduction. By 2014, Germany had reduced GHG emissions by 27 percent from 1990 levels.

While Germany is still the sixth highest GHG emitter globally (after the People's Republic of China, United States, India, the Russian Federation, and Japan), its current lead in climate actions is worth emulating. For one, Germany defies the perception that GHG emissions are an intrinsic part of economic growth. Patterns from 1991 show Germany successfully dissociating emissions from growth, as opposed to the global trend.

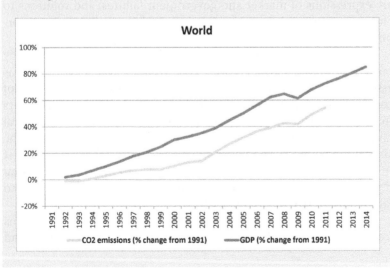

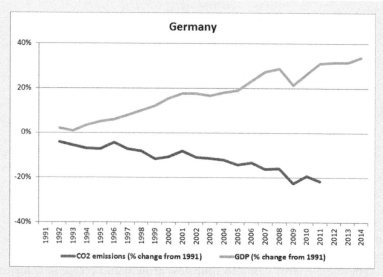

Source: WB WDI.

By 2050, the country aims to reduce GHG emissions further by 80 percent–95 percent from 1990 levels. Germany also aims to increase renewables' share in electricity consumption from 23 percent in 2013 to 80 percent in 2050. Germany's climate program pushes for urban renewal and for buildings to be carbon neutral by 2050. In particular:

- Germany's feed-in tariffs—government set price for renewable energy—helped create an attractive environment for renewables. With the policy ensuring a positive return-on-investments, long contracts, and access to the grid, local communities were encouraged to invest in renewables. By 2013, more than half of investments in renewables were made by small investors and local cooperatives.
- With over 90 percent of the population supporting renewables, German political parties are swayed to promote the transition to a renewable-based economy.

As Germany begins to reap the benefits of its huge infrastructure investments, the country demonstrates the positive influences of shifting to low-carbon systems to its economy:

- Taking advantage of improving energy efficiency and decreasing costs of renewables, energy costs are being lowered. Not only are Germany's industries benefiting from these lower energy costs, Germany is also attracting energy-intensive industries.
- As renewables replace energy imports, Germany's trade balance is expected to improve. This also lessens Germany's reliance on energy

imports and makes the country less vulnerable to the fluctuations of the world fossil-fuel market.

- Jobs in renewables have increased from fewer than two hundred thousand in 2005, to more than 370,000 in 2011.
- Local communities investing in and earning from renewables, strengthen local economies.
- Germany gains a first-mover advantage in the global market with its development of high-value engineering technologies, skills, and services in energy efficiency and renewables.

Sources: BMUB 2015; Handrich et al. 2015; Morris and Pehnt 2015; WB WDI Database.

Several steps can be taken that are conducive to economic growth and environmental sustainability. Slashing fossil-fuel subsidies amounting to over $500 billion a year globally is one example. Investments in renewable energy can also spur new growth and create new forms of employment. Reduced deforestation and reforestation can reduce the risks of flooding, landsides, and storm surges, as well as provide livelihood opportunities.

As countries restructure their economies to comply with sustainable and responsible practices, the misguided belief in a negative correlation between environmental care and economic growth could begin to disappear. The establishment of marine sanctuaries and ending of destructive practices such as dynamite and cyanide fishing in the fishing communities of Apo and Sumilon islands in the Philippines is a demonstration of this. The fishing communities themselves, together with the local governments and a local university, continue to protect the sanctuaries after witnessing increases in marine catch and size, and other associated economic benefits, including tourism (White et al. 2006).

In bridging the disconnect between knowledge and action that hinders the switch to a green economy, education plays an important role. The benefits of climate action and environmental protection do not accrue exclusively, directly, and linearly to those who act, but could spill across communities and national boundaries over time. Changing mindsets through education—about the physical repercussions of actions and, more importantly, toward sustainability and responsibility—can make a big difference.

Current and future generations must change how they price their actions, and how they price the associated present and future impacts of climate change, natural hazards, and disasters. It is about internalizing the costs of mitigation and adaptation, and how these costs will be many times greater in the future because of actions or inaction today. Higher GHG concentrations and a more wasted environment will intensify impacts and hazards.

In the same vein, political leaders must understand that action on climate change and natural disasters is a call to protect natural capital as an investment and not as a cost, and doing so will not jeopardize growth. They need to be informed that competitive pressures will unleash new technological changes and new jobs, and to realize that pressures to go green may soon become among the benchmarks of economic, social, and political strength.

The question remains: why are politicians not putting more effort into reducing disaster risks and into preparing more proactively for more regular and fierce climate-induced natural disasters? First, DRR and prevention are not as newsworthy and not as politically attractive as disaster response, relief, and reconstruction. Second, the benefits of DRR and prevention are neither as tangible nor as easy to quantify. The benefits of DRR and prevention may also accrue long after the expiry of the terms of current politicians, gaining them zero political mileage.

An aware and politicized electorate may be able to change this political equation. An interesting case is the People's Republic of China, which was forced recently to react positively to mass protests against pollution. Despite the political limits to dissent, highly passionate groups were able to voice their concerns and compel the government to take action.

Politics of Climate Mitigation

During much of the past two decades, international climate change agreements took a backseat and remained irrelevant. The Kyoto Protocol, the first international agreement stipulated to cut global GHG emissions, was not ratified by the United States. The protocol also exempted big developing countries like the People's Republic of China and India. By the end of the first commitment period in 2012, Canada, Japan, and the Russian Federation had already withdrawn from the agreement (RTCC 2015). And with the biggest emitters not covered, the protocol was deemed a failure by many.

From the 1992 Earth Summit in Rio de Janeiro to the 1997 Kyoto Protocol, GHG emissions continued to rise, as the treaties were neither binding nor acceptable to the biggest emitters. The 2009 summit in Copenhagen and the 2012 conference in Doha seem to have suffered a similar fate. According to Kingsnorth (2014) "[t]oday, carbon dioxide emissions are at record levels and rising, and no one appears to be willing or able to control them."

The International Energy Agency envisages that the Intended Nationally Determined Contributions received during the COP21 in Paris will fail to check global temperatures. Climate action based on the submitted pledges will increase global temperature by 2.7°C instead of the agreed target of 2.0°C by 2100 (IEA 2015).

Multilateral and international agreements have had a failed history. The main reason is that they face the free-rider problem. Since the impacts of global emissions are nonexcludable, that is, individuals can benefit from the good without contributing or paying for it, the free-rider problem arises. Everybody else shifting to a low-carbon path will benefit even those who continue to practice unsustainable activities. This rationale may be especially used by minor emitters—thinking that their emissions are negligible in the face of the bigger picture.

Countries have not wanted to do more than their perceived fair share through direct GHG reduction programs; and countries have not wanted to act proactively and enthusiastically in international agreements.

Some have even tried to steer international economic agreements in favor of domestic fossil-fuel industries. Others have managed to win international concessions that benefit the climate through short-term and low-cost actions in areas such as deforestation and forest fires.

A complete change of mindset is needed—away from "us-versus-them" or the "you-first" negotiations. All countries need to act and all need to cooperate to move toward low-carbon paths and sustainability.

Countries can benefit from unilateral action, with an eye toward enhancing their credibility in the international arena. Unilateral action is shielded from international politics and bureaucratic webs. And, in nonsymbolic terms, developing countries could take unilateral action without waiting for multilateral accords, especially when local and global gains overlap.

This was true of trade liberalization among developing countries in the past three decades, with a series of compelling studies bringing out the local benefits of trade reforms and action. The countries made progress on unilateral reform, to their own benefit, while multilateral negotiations stalled.

Climate reform could follow a similar path. Countries have been constrained politically by an incremental approach, which nudges each to give up a little carbon emission in a tit-for-tat manner. As a result, "emissions are rising, not falling . . . the global oil industry is having a field day—fracking, drilling, exploring in the Arctic, gasifying coal and building new liquefied natural gas facilities" (Sachs 2014).

Whatever may be the specific strategy for ushering in green growth—through international institutional arrangements, unilateral steps, or both—countries must act. Countries must not wait for international agreements that get mired in nationalist and political webs. And they cannot rely only on unilateral actions as these, without a global pact, will fall short. Multilateral agreements, when they do come about, will underpin own actions.

Some countries also continue to stand up to the West as a way to demonstrate their toughness on equity. Acceptance of international agreements is sometimes held back in order to appear tough during domestic elections. At the same time, India is also trying to please its own progressive constituencies by taking a less belligerent position—by taking unilateral steps to increase renewable energy production based on voluntary goals, as a way to reduce the carbon intensity of its economy.

Internationally mandated referendums could help countries understand the level and intensity of public support for climate action and the management of natural disasters. But the problem of turning referendums into binding environmental legislation rests partly on the fact that different countries have different constitutional interpretations of what referendums mean. In Belgium, for example, sovereignty rests with the nation, and not with the people. Since referendums are different expressions of direct democracy, they can run into a Belgium-like situation of becoming irrelevant.

Equally important is that referendums on climate change can be replaced or undermined by subsequent ones, creating a policy quagmire and an impediment to acting urgently. Not surprisingly, most countries continue to put faith in democratic elections to solve problems that are either unpopular or that are created partly by political leaders themselves.

The most important prerequisites for success were enabling or binding legal mandates, and a critical mass of businesses not fiercely hostile to green production processes. The European Union experience shows no robust correlations between governments that adopt significant green policies and the extent to which public priorities are articulated through the democratic process (EBRD 2011). While perceptions of political leaders may be misaligned with those of the electorate, an enlightened leadership may also act as climate stewards.

Highly vulnerable countries like Bangladesh, Maldives, and the Philippines have invoked the issue of staggering costs of climate-related disasters in election campaigns. More generally, political parties in democracies realize that failure to act on climate change and natural disasters can be blamed on a wide range of issues, from obscure institutional factors, administrative lapses, to the priorities of people themselves. Governments, therefore, continue to remain unaccountable, despite election promises on the climate and disaster prevention.

Paradoxically, governments like the People's Republic of China are more likely to be taken to task since they cannot pass the buck of climate inaction onto political opponents or onto politically independent institutions and unregulated practices. Astute political parties have tried to diversify their political base by promoting green-technologies as a national economic strategy. Germany is perhaps an example of this successful electoral strategy, which has actually lived up to its promise. But the opposite is often the case, despite the presence of watchdogs such as a vibrant and independent media and nonstate actors such as nongovernment organizations.

The climate problem is framed, if at all, in very narrow terms during election campaigns. Politicians in a predominantly rural country like India constantly talk about rural development, without ever mentioning the effect of climate change on rainfall and therefore on agricultural prices.

The idea of cobenefits of climate change seems to be gaining ground, analogous to the dissemination of findings on benefits of growth that had ignited the progress made on investments in health. Several studies, including the World Development Report 2003, made the case for health (World Bank 2003b), and they became the bases for investments by international financial institutions as well as private entities such as the Bill and Melinda Gates Foundation.

Comparisons of present costs and future gains could similarly be the foundation of reform and investment for climate mitigation. The health benefits of reduced pollution are the most obvious examples. They can be folded into electoral campaigns when the electorate cares about health and other immediate issues, rather than long-term and single-point issues like climate change.

Political leaders will act on major climate change problems when the pressure comes either from a seemingly disengaged electorate, or from the enlightened self-interest of the political class to gain relative autonomy from the fossil-fuel industry. For the former to happen, the electorate has to be mobilized, politicized, and re-motivated—a massive task that has rarely succeeded. And for the latter to become a reality, political elites in developing countries must be shown that a greener quality of life is also in their own self-interest.

The growth aspects of the environment need to be highlighted to create a broad political base. To address the concerns of the electorate and political leaders at the same time, the very short-term benefits of climate mitigation and adaptation must therefore be translated into tangible benefits, like lower fuel bills, green jobs, and a major reduction in health problems.

Energy efficiency as a mitigation option works, as demonstrated by the members of the International Energy Agency and the Group of Twenty. In the United States, energy use per US dollar was cut in half in the last thirty-five years from 12.1 thousand British thermal units per US dollar in 1980 to 6.1 thousand British thermal units per US dollar in 2014. This does not only translate into lower consumption and emissions, but also into lower fuel bills which amounted to about $800 billion in 2014, roughly $2,500 per capita (American Council for an Energy-Efficient Economy 2015). This evidence should be easy to translate into a public concern and eventually, policy.

The People's Republic of China's outdoor air and water pollution was estimated to cost the country some $100 billion a year in heath and non-health costs (World Bank 2007a). Given the convergence of the demands of the electorate and a growth imperative, the Chinese government has scaled up its investments in renewables, adding more toward wind and photovoltaics than in the coal sector.

Globally, one in eight deaths, or some 3.7 million deaths in 2012, were attributed to outdoor air pollution (WHO n.d.). Considering that 88 percent of these deaths occur in low and middle income countries, it is clearly a developmental and public health concern.

Another way to think about environment as an election issue is to understand that politicians find it hard to renounce assured funding from entrenched fossil-fuel constituencies for new votes from the environment sector. In the run up to the United States 2016 elections, climate change received no mention from the numerous candidates for the nomination of the Republican Party. Politicians evaluate whether climate mitigation poses a risk or presents an opportunity. If problems are projected as merely administrative that could be addressed through the departments of environment or energy, then politically risky climate action is often rendered a nonpolitical issue that is then taken out of the electoral arena.

The result is political apathy from above and below, and a status quo perpetuated by fossil-fuel lobbies, where carbon-intensive industries, as the biggest export earners, the biggest taxpayers, and the biggest employers, end up calling the shots. However, with the prices of renewables falling, the political calculus in the electoral arena may change significantly, and political parties may find it far easier to make promises on the climate front than on intractable ones like poverty alleviation.

Whether environmental issues are election-winning issues or not may have a lot to do with coalition politics. Australia illustrates this dynamic. When Australian Labor candidate, Julia Gillard, ran for prime minister in 2010, she had explicitly ruled out the idea of a carbon tax—primarily because she didn't have enough strength in her coalition in Parliament to win. She was therefore forced to make a deal with the Green Party, including an understanding on moving with a carbon tax. After winning the elections with support from the Greens, Gillard pushed the carbon tax idea forcefully and legislated it in 2012.

In the meantime, political opponents showed successfully that GHGs had already dropped (without the legislation), and that polluters had already behaved responsibly (without mentioning the cushioning effect of subsidies). They pledged a repeal of the tax if voted in power. Without the pressures of a coalition government, the conservative candidate Tony Abbott managed to get the tax repealed. In the process he won the elections.

A lesson from the Australian example is the necessity of institutionalizing binding agreements on basic climate issues that is relatively immune from changes in government. In that sense, critical climate action may indeed be taken out of the electoral arena.

However, the democratic ideal of the people's voice making a difference continues to have sway. A United Kingdom poll in 2014 for instance, celebrated the fact that 23 percent of the nation's citizens saw climate change as the number one problem the country faced (Barasi

2014). Record-breaking floods and storms had undoubtedly influenced the judgment.

Although politicians of all stripes echoed that sentiment, there was no consensus on the specifics. Should we push aggressively on funding renewables, stop fracking, or spend more on flood defense systems? Expressing preferences through the electoral arena may not be enough to bring about meaningful climate action.

The 2013 elections in Washington State's Whatcom County attracted a million US dollars in outside donations, and zeroed in on a controversial coal export facility. All candidates supporting the environment won. The reason behind the success was the combination of money and mobilization. Mainstream environmental groups established a robust grassroots presence and, together with political action committees, leveraged millions to make climate change the key electoral issue (Carpenter 2013).

Nothing can be assumed about the outcome of election processes, even when climate change appears to be a losing proposition at the outset, and even if directly at odds with a strong energy industry. Through a combination of enabling legislations, co-benefits, and aggressive fundraising and mobilization, climate change may be able to compete with other issues in the electoral arena.

Carbon Strategies and Technological Fixes

Mitigation calls for switching to renewable energy on a significant scale, energy efficiency, reducing emissions from all economic activities, and capturing the harmful residues through carbon sequestration technologies. Adaptation policies, on the other hand, call for learning to cope with climate impacts even as mitigation policies are being pursued.

On the mitigation front, the shift to clean energy could most efficiently be achieved by imposing a carbon tax. But carbon taxes must be backed by new legislation, which unfortunately vested interests would resist fiercely. This political economy approach would seek to mobilize the support of industries and political leaders on the basis of neutrality, efficiency, and equity in taxes across GHGs, sectors, and business types. For instance, political opposition will be less severe if all uses of fossil fuels faced the same tax per unit of emission (Jenkins 2014).

Successful mitigation policies would have to pay attention to differences in resistance from different communities and different energy industries. By disaggregating political dynamics in this way, tax revenues (or a reduction in carbon subsidies) can be spent successfully in a targeted way to spur growth and address environmental issues. Political acceptance of unpopular environmental programs can be enhanced by linking them with co-benefits, such as health, national or energy security, jobs, or disaster prevention.

The contentious debate on using tax revenues revolves around forcing industries to pay for carbon emissions through taxes. Given the stance of rapidly industrializing countries such as the People's Republic of China and India, a global carbon tax seems like a political nonstarter. The skeptical view is that carbon taxes will not even cover the costs of basic infrastructure improvements in most countries.

Political leaders are reluctant to promote taxes that are unpopular to begin with. Even the pro-environment party of Canada rejected a carbon tax. But the experience of Nordic countries suggests that well-implemented energy taxes can win public and political approval, particularly when carbon taxes are proclaimed to spur growth and catalyze investments, rather than cover the entire costs of modernization and all climate change programs.

Legislation that influences carbon prices can be hijacked readily by organized lobby groups representing fossil-fuel industries. By winning subsidies in the form of trade exemptions, carbon credits, and other offsets, the efficiency and environmental benefits of carbon pricing may be undermined.

The idea could be to recycle carbon revenues for people's well-being as carbon subsidies drop. Even then, political opposition may emerge as the societal benefits of mitigation may not be aligned with the private costs incurred by consumers and citizens in different areas at different times. The difficulty of slashing carbon subsidies lies in the fact that the price of carbon-intensive products go up in the short term. The costs associated with carbon policies can be significant, enough to be resisted if those committed to environmental issues are not leveraged and sufficiently mobilized. Many climate advocates have begun to lobby political leaders for better uses of revenues generated by reducing carbon subsidies or by increasing carbon taxes.

The failure to mobilize support against fossil-fuel subsidies clarifies political economy constraints in the sharpest way. Some of the largest financial benefits from subsidies go to powerful industrial interests that lobby to defend them. For wealthy and middle class households, subsidies help lower the costs of living, thus generating a vocal and powerful constituency against a low-carbon policy.

Poor households are also implicated if energy prices go up as energy comprises a large share of their spending. In the case of farmers, removing subsidies may also raise the price of fertilizers and other agricultural inputs. Political economy constraints therefore echo throughout society, and it is not difficult to see why many policy makers increasingly pin their hopes on the magic of disinterested environmental technologies.

A strong bureaucracy, riding on the success of its past achievements, can have the capacity to override political constraints in the struggle to implement climate change policies. What is becoming increasingly important is to implement existing laws and technologies on a larger scale rather than searching endlessly for new sources of green technologies and green growth. If prices of new technologies can go down, political barriers will go down too.

With government backing, the People's Republic of China's photovoltaic industries have become the largest players in the world. The country stands to gain much from the prestige inherent in the role of a leader in new climate technologies.

In the United States, the Environmental Protection Agency has achieved success in reducing air pollution, cleaning water, and banning the use of DDT. As a result of existing laws and technologies, administrators believe there would be relatively less political opposition if the Environmental Protection Agency expanded its existing role and capacity to take on climate change.

In 2007, the US Supreme Court asked the Environmental Protection Agency to find a link between GHGs and human health. The Environmental Protection Agency then submitted a scientific report showing how CO_2 and five other GHGs threatened health because they caused global warming. According to legislations, the Environmental Protection Agency was bound to formulate regulations to deal with the health-climate change problems, and it set about establishing them for cars, trucks, and new power plants (but not for existing power plants and many other major sources of pollution). Resistance from many quarters followed.

If the Environmental Protection Agency had instead gone through a less cumbersome process and implemented its successful Clean Air Act, it would have imposed *de facto* a successful carbon tax and a gradual reversal of carbon subsidies. The Clean Air Act could have achieved a 40 percent reduction of GHG emissions over 1990 levels by 2020 (Parenti 2013).

Governments must catalyze markets for green technologies and renewables by creating the demand for them in their procurements, by mandating the use of renewable energy products in all government institutions, and by drastically improving the energy efficiency of all public facilities. Governments are major market players and can influence and leverage their procurement policies without changing taxes and spending details. Political constraints in a shift toward green products and green growth will be relatively minimal. The United States federal government is the world's largest consumer of energy and vehicles. If it shifts into renewables and low-carbon technology, markets and businesses will be driven into the green and clean path (Parenti 2013).

Governments are also uniquely positioned to legislate and enforce quotas on the amount of fossil fuels that may be extracted. The story of the Environmental Protection Agency showed this process in the case of clean air and clean water. An enlightened bureaucracy can be blamed for short-term adverse consequences; and credited for mid-term positive outcomes.

Consider, also, market instruments like the cap-and-trade systems. The Clean Development Mechanism was institutionalized to meet the emission reduction targets under the Kyoto Protocol. This arrangement allows emission reduction projects in developing countries to earn certified emission reduction credits which can be traded and sold. These credits are used by industrialized countries to help meet their emission targets. While the mechanism is supposed to help meet the development needs of developing countries and reduce emissions, the policy instrument instead had legitimized the growth of carbon emissions (Bohm and Dabhi 2009).

The market-based system turned GHG emissions into commodities that were affected by hoarding and speculation. In the United States, heavy corporate lobbying made the scheme very friendly to corporations (Giddens 2009). Big emitters received huge caps and received windfall profits by selling carbon credits in the market, and helped maintain the status quo.

The largest buyers of emission credits are speculators on Wall Street and other major financial markets. These financiers and institutions have invested millions in lobbying for offsets. Assisted by carbon brokers, bureaucrats, and their political backers, investors expand trade with limited or even adverse effects on emissions reduction.

The surge in natural gas and oil production, enabled partly by hydraulic fracturing and horizontal drilling, has made the United States the world's largest oil producer and a dominant player in global energy markets. Thirty-five years ago, the situation had been very different, since the United States had little control over energy prices. Set in the driver's seat, the United States is more positioned to influence the global energy markets and climate action.

The goal of influencing carbon or energy markets through the promotion of green technologies or renewables appears politically more acceptable today. Subsidization of research and development is part of an optimal policy to reduce emissions (Akerlof 2014). Research has been focusing on developing safe and efficient carbon storage technologies. They have the possibility of harnessing effluents from clean energy sources and reducing fossil-fuel emissions into the atmosphere and the seas. Proponents of such laboratory approaches therefore believe that political interference in research and development will be manageable and lead to outcomes that are more acceptable to business leaders, nongovernment organizations, and the voters themselves.

But scientific communities fear the unintended consequences of technological fixes on climate and natural ecologies. For example, no one knows how iron-seeding of oceans or creating oceanic algae may affect marine and fish life as a whole; how sequestering carbon in the soil may impact food supplies and bacterial life; or how shooting sulfur or seeding and scattering clouds to deflect sunlight may interfere with planetary forces. Except for promising advances in the carbon capture and storage arena,[1] almost all technology fixes could lead governments to the portals of another set of international problems, requiring more complex international agreements involving the seas and the skies, than that engendered by carbon emissions.

Underinvestment in Disaster Risk Reduction[2]

Despite known risks, investments to prevent the loss of growth-inducing assets, protect global manufacturing chains, or to boost investor confidence have remained inadequate. Recurring disasters are threatening to erode the progress in poverty reduction, especially in Asia and the Pacific.

Acting ahead of a natural disaster through DRR measures or insurance allows governments access to earmarked funds without diverting resources from other programs. Vulnerable households also are freed from the burden of saving or keeping money aside specifically for disasters. Insurance schemes work best when the public sector sets up the insurance pool's regulatory framework, raises awareness, and provides input to the institutional design of the pool. Such prospects are promising motivational factors for politicians, and allow them to act unilaterally in order to capture benefits from new disaster-related markets such as disaster risk management.

Political leaders can sell disaster prevention as part of a green growth strategy to elicit a broader appeal. They can also clarify in stark terms the costs and the immense benefits of disaster management measures and disaster insurance. The Caribbean Catastrophe Risk Insurance Facility and the Turkish Catastrophe Insurance Pool Fund Program are cited as potentially successful initiatives between insurers, governments, and donors—which could be scaled up significantly if the right amount of political will was available.[3]

Most countries regard these extreme events purely as acts of nature. It is in this context that communities and people remain passive, with very little effort at prevention and preparedness. Disasters are not part of the economic and growth agenda: disasters are seen not to hurt growth, and disaster prevention is not seen to sustain growth. The political implication is denial and inaction.

Since prevention continues to be ranked low on the priority list, politicians break down disaster preparedness projects into smaller parts, in favor of much larger infrastructure projects. In addition, the enormity of effort required to combat natural disasters in a systematic way forces political leaders to address disaster issues in a gradual or piecemeal way, leading to success in some areas and failures in others.

Governments underinvest because they do not want to spend when they do not think disasters are imminent. The inherent mix of market and government failures in disaster prevention results in poor DRR, and consequently huge disaster losses. Yet, disaster damage varies greatly across countries, and a comparative analysis can reveal why a poor country (like Bangladesh) can invest heavily and successfully in disaster preparedness, whereas much more affluent countries cannot or do not.

Underinvestment in DRR and prevention can also be explained by an attitude of calculated indifference among political leaders. Since most governments and their bureaucracies can absorb the costs of disaster damages over time, the urgency to act recedes. As the memory of disasters fade, those affected by disasters within a specific region are not necessarily the ones who matter most in broader elections. So politicians may not capitalize on destructive natural disasters and take appropriate action.

An understanding of why some governments are more capable than others in responding to natural disasters reveals underlying constraints. In 2010, a 7.0 magnitude earthquake hit Haiti, killing 222,000 people. A far stronger earthquake (8.8 magnitude) hit Chile but fewer than a thousand were killed. Although strict building codes helped, the government immediately reached out to international institutions, for investing in the poor who had been the worst hit. In contrast, a weak government in Haiti, with no building codes, barely managed to respond. Given a political vacuum, government officials found it easy to siphon disaster aid. Violent protests against elites had no effect. Some argue that Chile was better able to prepare and respond because it is more developed, while Haiti is the western hemisphere's poorest country. But Chile is more developed because it is doing things right with the rule of law and accountability, education, and administrative efficiency (Padgett 2010).

Similarly, effective disaster response rests on government ability to invest in disaster preparedness. The 2001 Peru earthquake that led to fewer than 150 deaths was far stronger than the one in 1970 when sixty-six thousand people were killed. The difference was that in 2001 the country had a democratic system with a vibrant and free media. In contrast, Peru did not have a democratic system in 1970. Put simply, Peru's political elites in 1970 were unaccountable and faced almost no political economy constraints to act and invest responsibly or irresponsibly.

Floods in 2014 in Assam in India reveal opportunities for political corruption (Mukhim 2014). Relief operations after the flood were fraught with red tape, corruption, and pilferage. Politicians, bureaucrats, and disaster workers who stand to benefit from delays ensure that the disaster response drags on as much as possible.

Politics often constrain disaster response. In recent times, the decision by the People's Republic of China to dam the Tsangpo River, which becomes the Brahmaputra when it enters India, has generated concerns for the sustainable use of water. Hydrologists claim that this could have two effects. One, the Brahmaputra could recede and shrink in size. Second, there could be a cloudburst from the release of excess water, and people downstream could face negative impacts.

The People's Republic of China shares hydrological information during the monsoons, but with climate change making so many things so unpredictable, perhaps an hourly data sharing between the People's Republic of China and India might help Assam better cope with floods.

If there are political constraints to sharing information among countries, investments in disaster management suffer.

Since the politics of natural disasters are also manifested locally, governments have to make choices about who to help and who not to help, who should take credit for recovery and reconstruction, and what specific benefits are doled out and to whom. The visibility of relief efforts provides incentives to governments to sell recovery and reconstruction programs as poverty alleviation projects, with co-benefits in areas such as health, employment, and overall security. What limits their ability to invest in disaster management is the intensity of protests that may follow when governments do not respond appropriately after disasters.

Most governments put aside some funds for disaster response. However, they find themselves in the typical fire fighter position—that is, they don't boost their skills or investments when there are no fires (or disasters). This aspect of disaster management seriously affects the investment leaders will put toward disaster preparedness and disaster risk management.

The poor are most vulnerable as they are not able to avoid disaster cost. Poor settlements in both urban and rural areas are often found in high-risk areas where buildings and infrastructure are not resilient to climate change. Homes of the poor are most likely to be damaged or completely destroyed when hazards strike.

With the blessing of local political leaders, real estate developers and affluent farmers are able to indirectly push the poor to low-cost and hazardous areas. Since natural hazards cannot be exactly predicted, people tend to neglect or ignore risks, and expect a government response when disasters strike. Local governments also remain unengaged.

The private sector underinvests in disaster preparation and mitigation. Disaster insurance markets in many countries, particularly poorer economies, remain undeveloped. Hence, private infrastructure in poor countries are likely to be uninsured. Where disaster insurance is available, coverage may be limited as certain disaster types, as well as high-risk areas are not covered. Insurance policies also often come with high premiums for disaster coverage, which may discourage the private sector from availing of such protection.

Insurance does not reduce the total economic cost of natural disasters (Neumayer et al. 2014). Often, insurance policies require that the insured individual or company engage in disaster prevention before the insurance releases any payout. Often, the opposite is the case. Poor but insured individuals may put little effort into disaster loss prevention, specifically because of the knowledge that they are insured. This market failure can be something that governments can perhaps resolve.

Government budget constraints explain why they underinvest in disaster prevention and management. Disaster-proofing of public infrastructure may be effective for some natural hazards such as earthquakes and hurricanes only.

Government regulation and investment can play a key role. Government policy together with effective implementation can limit settlements and discourage livelihoods in high-risk areas. Strict enforcement of disaster-proof building standards can ensure climate-resilient private infrastructure. Governments can also take the lead in collective infrastructure investments such as dams and dykes, flood control and management, early warning systems, and mass housing in low-risk areas. Priorities in government expenditure is once again the limiting factor.

Large-scale disasters cause significant collateral damages that impact the wider population. However, governments are not particularly motivated to internalize these costs, because natural disasters continue to be treated in a non-systemic way and with low priority.

While private investments in disaster preparedness and loss mitigation are riddled by market failures, governments could step in to act in the interest of the public good. In a sense, governments exert a strong influence on disaster costs (Neumayer et al. 2014). Publicly provided infrastructure such as highways, airports, seaports, and utilities such as power and water facilities are often adversely affected by natural hazards. Governments determine the quality of these infrastructure and consequently, the cost of post-disaster reconstruction and rehabilitation.

Apart from budget constraints, governments underinvest in disaster management for political reasons (Neuymayer et al. 2014). Politicians decide on government projects which can help them win political support from constituents. One option is to invest in disaster-proofed infrastructure which can help increase political support in the event of a severe natural disaster. Another option is to provide short-term solutions with immediate impact to society and can help win political support in the immediate-term. The latter appears to be true for most countries, and therefore governments end up underinvesting in disaster preparedness and mitigation.

Neumayer et al. (2014) gives the example of the small city of Fudai on the northeast coast of Japan. They narrated that in the 1960s, the government built a sixteen-meter high concrete wall to protect the city from tsunamis. During that time, city mayor Wamura was criticized for wasting public resources. This investment in disaster mitigation proved effective around five decades later when the wall protected Fudai from the tsunami that arose after the March 2011 earthquake. Fudai's three thousand inhabitants were spared while other nearby villages, which built only smaller dams, were washed over by the tsunami.

Governments avoid making unpopular policies such as a prohibition on buildings and settlements in high-risk areas. Mandating and enforcing building standards are also perceived as an additional burden on private individuals, serving little purpose in the absence of a disaster.

The proposed Sustainable Development Goals demonstrate how DRR is interlinked with human well-being and development. Given how disasters push people into hardship and poverty, achieving Sustainable Development Goal targets will be challenging for some countries if DRR is not prioritized. In the domain of the Sustainable Development Goals, underinvestment in DRR is not an option.

Role of Multilateral Development Banks

Organizations such as the Asian Development Bank, the International Monetary Fund, and the World Bank, together with country partners, seek to foster economic and social progress in countries. With the rising threat of climate change, the effectiveness of their work stands or falls on solutions they can bring to confront the environmental threat. Traditionally set up to do loans, the multilateral development banks need new and innovative instruments and approaches to address climate change.

The rising frequency of natural disasters affects economic growth and poverty reduction, the overarching goals of multilateral development banks.

Without DRR, preparedness, and prevention, including climate adaptation and mitigation, their development agenda will suffer setbacks. Against this perspective, these institutions have a long way to go in promoting, leveraging, and delivering policies and investments for a low-carbon global economy.

Acknowledging that disasters can threaten years of progress, multilateral development banks feature DRR centrally in their development policies. They are also urging governments to incorporate DRR, preparedness, and adaptation into their national plans and to increase investment in these areas.

Until recently, multilateral development banks focused on providing countries with financial and technical support for disaster response and post-disaster reconstruction. As climate-related disasters become more frequent, however, they are beginning to work toward DRR, disaster prevention, and climate resilience (World Bank 2012b).

Multilateral development banks are also helping countries shift to low-carbon development. They have been promoting and supporting GHG accounting, energy efficiency, renewable energy development, emissions reduction, climate change adaptation, and the reduction of fossil-fuel subsidies and stabilizing carbon prices (Nakhooda 2008). The World Bank and the Asian Development Bank have supported carbon pricing as a strategy for enhancing productivity in energy markets and to reduce emissions.

The World Bank is one of the major international funding institutions and research conduits for climate change-related development work. It has made investments in clean energy and climate-related projects, as well as disaster prevention. In 2015, the World Bank Group reported making 188 climate change-related investments in fifty-nine countries, ranging from helping farmers adapt to a changing climate, to new investments in renewable energy. The World Bank is also a leader in disaster risk management, and helped over a hundred million people in fifty countries gain improved access to risk information.

The Asian Development Bank has delivered climate mitigation and adaptation projects in Asia and the Pacific, promoting access for the region's poor to low-carbon energy sources and sustainable transportation, while promoting energy efficiency. Its adaptation program works to safeguard national development strategies, strengthen vulnerable sectors, climate proof infrastructure projects, and address social impacts of climate change. The bank has set environmentally sustainable development as a center piece of its strategy in Asia and the Pacific.

Inter-American Development Bank for its part has identified the protection of the environment, response to climate change, and promotion of renewable energy as some of its top priorities. Inter-American Development Bank's climate-related lending averaged 19 percent of the Bank's total portfolio in the period 2004–2013. The Bank focused more on climate mitigation than adaptation, with energy and transport projects dominating the climate change portfolio. While Inter-American Development Bank's disaster risk management activities are aligned with the region's risk levels, the Bank does not draw the links between climate adaptation and disaster risk management. The governments then tend to focus on disaster response, leaving climate change implications in disaster risk management unattended (Gonzalez et al. 2014).

The European Bank for Reconstruction and Development addresses climate change mitigation through its Sustainable Energy Initiative which invests in energy efficiency projects in industrial processes, transmission networks, renewable energy, and municipal infrastructure such as district heating, transport networks, and water supply systems. To complement this Initiative, the Bank began integrating climate change adaptation in its investment operations. Since 2010, the Bank reports providing climate change adaptation finance through seventy-eight projects in twenty countries. In Tajikistan, water supply systems were upgraded to make them more resilient to changing climate. In Romania and Ukraine, water-efficient technologies were introduced to agri-processing firms. In Georgia, climate change assessments were integrated into Environmental and Social Impact Assessment in the expansion of a major port which is vulnerable to potential sea level rises and changes in sedimentation patterns.

Multilateral development banks have increased their scope to accommodate climate change mitigation and adaptation, as well as DRR. But far more needs to be done to minimize human and physical losses, and disruptions in productive activities. To remain relevant in development and to help secure the gains of growth in the midst of a changing climate, multilateral development banks need to scale up climate action. Multilateral development banks are also in place to have a stronger stance and more compelling leadership in climate action.

Constraints to Scaling-Up Climate Action

Multilateral development banks face institutional and funding constraints in responding to the challenges of climate change and climate-related disasters. Their own lack of advisory and technical capacities to administer climate finance diminishes demand for mitigation and adaptation.

Bottlenecks in technology development, legalities, and conflicting interests may slow the pace of climate initiatives. Questions of economic or commercial-scale viability, as well as safety issues, may limit acceptability. And smart land-use planning, a powerful instrument for reducing hazards, is often constrained by overlapping, informal, and questionable property rights, particularly in vulnerable urban slums.

Multilateral development banks are bound to work within the legal frameworks and priorities of recipient countries, which may temper the best-intentioned policy advice or efforts. Despite the foreboding impacts of climate change, climate action may still not feature high on government agendas.

Politics can interrupt climate action. While the governments of Indonesia and the Republic of Korea are putting climate change policies, along with ambitious targets, into their political agenda, many developing countries are reluctant to cut emissions (Freeman III and Searight 2010). Country leaders may be uneasy about the possible economic repercussions of capping emissions since these can be traced back to them. Politicians recognize that people are unwilling to pay more for emissions reduction even if it is beneficial to everyone. And no government is willing to raise the costs of doing business and lose in the world economy. Except for the European countries, few others have enthusiastically raised fossil-fuel costs or set emissions limits.

Far More Can Be Done in Policy

Multilateral development banks, as well as regional and bilateral development organizations, can do more to internalize climate change action into their own decision-making and operations. While multilateral development banks acknowledge the need to mainstream climate change action into their operations, over 60 percent of their energy sector financing still do not consider emissions (Nakhooda 2008).

Multilateral development banks should mainstream and incorporate disaster and climate risks into the design and implementation of regular investment operations. This implies, at the very least, that they should climate-proof their own work in the areas of growth and poverty reduction.

Multilateral development banks can strengthen their capacities to reposition themselves less as donors and more as repositories of knowledge and best development practices. And they can develop expertise in disaster risks and climate action as well as in the assessment of policies in these areas.

117

These organizations are also best placed to shift attention from the GHG emissions blame-game, to finding ways of dealing with the sources of the problem. The complexity of forging global agreements, and the dearth of country commitments toward sustainability (in the name of self-interest and growth), should provide the impetus for multilateral development banks to support a low-carbon growth path in countries, without waiting for international climate treaties. This would be analogous to their vigorous support for unilateral trade reforms, especially in the face of stalled multilateral negotiations.

The multilateral development banks can also play a vital role in supporting low-carbon strategies in developing member countries. Aside from demonstrating the economic viability of renewables, they can influence governments to address market failures in the environment. Through information and advocacy, multilateral development banks can demonstrate the social costs of fuel subsidies.

Given Asian Development Bank's focus on infrastructure, and the susceptibility of Asia and the Pacific to the impacts of climate change and climate-related disasters, adopting a climate-infrastructure strategy is a unique opportunity for Asian Development Bank to address one of the region's greatest challenges. Developing countries in Asia and the Pacific have also generally lagged behind other regions in disaster risk financing. The climate-infrastructure strategy would also tap into Asian Development Bank's strengths, promise high returns on the institution's portfolio, and give it a strategic and unique role in promoting development through climate actions. Box 6.2 presents seven considerations in this irresistible agenda.

Multilateral development banks should also play a more active role in coordinating regional climate action and initiatives for disaster resilience, as well as harmonizing standards and policies (Stern 2007).

Far More Influence Needed

Multilateral development banks should emphasize the need for countries to integrate climate change and disaster management with their development policies, as well as to invest systematically in the entire disaster management cycle.

They can present countries with different options to achieve short- and long-term goals in DRR. These will include a rigorous cost and benefit analysis of alternatives to achieve climate-resilient development. This naturally presupposes familiarity with GHG emissions accounting based on the valuation of natural capital and the climate vulnerability of a project area.

They can also build on the disaster risk assessments practiced by many primary insurance and reinsurance firms. The multilateral development banks should help institutionalize such knowledge and procedures in relevant departments in government ministries, including organizations further down the public hierarchy.

Multilateral development banks should identify how different areas, such as forests and other ecosystems, may respond to climatic variability regionally and globally. This will help reduce the vulnerability of people in risky zones and allow the multilateral development banks and governments to incorporate such knowledge into area development plans.

Box 6.2. The Asian Development Bank's role in climate action.

The implications of climate change for development in Asia and the Pacific are profound. The Asian Development Bank, with its special focus on infrastructure, is positioned to make a difference. The following seven considerations must be seized:

The climate threat: Asia has been hit disproportionately by climate-related floods, storms, heatwaves, and droughts, which threaten growth.

Asia's responsibility: Asia contributes 45 percent to global GHG emissions and Asia's middle-income countries have a disproportionate share (relative to its GDP) of GHG emissions that underlie global warming.

Sources of warming: The energy and transport sectors, which represent two-thirds of ADB's lending, are also responsible for two-thirds of global GHG emissions.

ADB's advantage: A stronger portfolio in climate-related investments in energy and transport than comparable organizations in the private and public sectors.

Regional response: Asian Development Bank's regional cooperation pillar provides an opening for regional climate actions.

Middle-income countries: The majority of Asian Development Bank's clients are going to be middle-income countries, and their participation in Asian Development Bank's portfolio will find strong justification in climate actions.

Financing leverage: With the availability of climate financing set to exceed its effective use, Asian Development Bank has the chance to leverage such funds.

Source: IED (2015).

Given the enormous knowledge bases they share with similar organizations, multilateral development banks are positioned to play this role in disaster prevention and risk management.

Much More Can Be Done in Finance

Since 2011, multilateral development banks have collectively committed over $100 billion to address climate change in developing and emerging economies.

In 2014, seven multilateral development banks[4] committed a reported $28 billion in climate finance, 91 percent of which came from their own resources, and the rest from other multilateral and bilateral donors (AfDB et al. 2015). This was equivalent, on average, to 22 percent of their total development financing. The World Bank delivered a reported $9.2 billion, equivalent to 23 percent of the Bank's total 2014 commitments. The European Bank for Reconstruction and Development earmarked more than a third of their 2014 commitments to climate finance. In 2015, Asian Development Bank announced its plans of doubling its annual climate finance from $3 billion to $6 billion by 2020, to make up 30 percent of its overall financing.

In 2014, almost 30 percent ($18 billion) of the $61.8 billion climate finance mobilized by developed countries for developing countries were sourced from multilateral development banks. An additional $8.6 billion was mobilized by multilateral development banks from private sources (OECD 2015).

Multilateral development banks should seize any opportunity to leverage the public and private sectors, as well as other development partners to manage critical risk areas. They can direct development funds to restore ecosystems such as forests, wetlands, and mangroves. They can leverage private finance for climate change, disaster risk management, and carbon markets. And through the wide range of financing instruments available to them, they can effectively steer governments and the private sector toward basic efficiencies in energy production and use.

In 2012, the Green Growth Action Alliance proposed that multilateral development banks design a standard renewable energy power purchase agreement for emerging markets and develop new insurance products to support investments in green infrastructure. By drawing finance from development and commercial banks, multilateral development banks can provide affordable capital for energy efficiency projects. They can also pool corporate demand for renewable energy.

Disaster risk financing can help reduce liquidity gaps that hamper the capacity of governments, households, and businesses to recover from disasters. Financial protection strategies include programs to increase the capacity of governments to respond to emergencies.

In the Caribbean, a regional catastrophe risk insurance facility has provided short-term liquidity to governments to better respond to emergency needs after severe hurricanes and earthquakes. In Mexico, a state-led fund for natural disasters has demonstrated that reinsurance and catastrophe bonds can be combined with sound budgetary practices to provide support to federal and state governments affected by natural disasters (IED 2012).

Being Better Prepared

The surge in floods and storms and the rise in heatwaves and droughts have not only inflicted enormous losses in lives and livelihood, but have also exacted a political price. In the United States, President George W. Bush's ratings nosedived because of the government's failure to assume responsibility after Hurricane Katrina. In Beijing, after losses mounted to $1.6 billion due to heavy rains and flooding in 2012, the local government found itself scurrying to control public opinion rather than dealing with disaster damage itself. The rising frequency of natural disasters can be ignored only at a significant political cost.

Governments seem to have woken up to the political and growth implications of working with new disaster insurance companies and risk markets. Management of endemic disaster risks could lead to a robust development of disaster insurance markets. Such markets could have the potential to catalyze other industry-wide investments or spur new economic activities, as in most developed countries.

Governments cannot prevent disaster damage entirely. Making buildings earthquake-proof can avert their collapse, but cannot prevent property damage within buildings when the ground shakes. Infrastructure and buildings that withstand collapse may still be damaged, as earthquakes cause structural cracks and other flaws that require extensive repair.

Worse still, earthquakes can trigger tsunamis, landslides, and fires, which are much more difficult to mitigate, let alone prevent. For example, a significant portion of the damage of Japan's two costliest earthquakes—the 1995 Kobe and the 2011 Tōhoku disasters—was caused not by the shaking of the ground, but by the fire and tsunami waves that followed. Government's investment in disaster insurance cannot anticipate the entire range of such complexities.

While climate-proofed buildings and other infrastructure may withstand the wind speed of a tropical storm, it is likely that those buildings will still incur damages. A glaring example is flood damage. With the underinvestment in a flood management system, the intake capacity of urban drainage systems will not be able to accommodate excessive rainfall during the monsoon season. In rural areas, heavy rainfall would cause the swelling of rivers and creeks, causing flooding in surrounding areas. Well-built and well-placed dykes and dams can channel the excess rainfall and avert the worst.

While disaster damages cannot be eliminated, they can be reduced with adaptation and preparedness. Though uncertainty is high, we can draw lessons and effective practices from past experiences.

Government policy cannot fully prevent damages from natural disasters. This is especially true in disaster prone countries. Even small-scale damages are sometimes unavoidable. Neumayer et al. (2014) presented the average estimated damage of minor earthquakes, those that register below 6.0 on the Richter scale, in countries with low propensity for earthquakes. They showed that the damages varied for no apparent reason, specifically $0.19 million damage in Spain, $10.6 million in Germany, and $16.2 million in the United Kingdom. They also argued that this is not significantly different from the average damage of $3.9 million caused by minor earthquakes in a highly vulnerable country like Japan.

Governments of highly vulnerable countries will find an incentive in enforcing policies that will mitigate large-scale damage of natural disasters. While these mitigating mechanisms may be in place, it is unfortunate that these same countries also have a higher likelihood of experiencing a one-off extreme disaster event. It is highly likely that these countries will experience an extreme disaster which will exceed its capacity for disaster preparedness and mitigation. For example, the damage brought about by Hurricane Katrina was about four times larger than the next most damaging hurricane in the preceding four decades, and at least one order of magnitude larger than the average damage of tropical storms of equivalent magnitude (Neumayer et al. 2014).

The fact that disaster damages cannot be eliminated adds to the premium on actions that reduce them. The unpredictability can be sobering and encourages realism. But the addition of human made causes adds to the sense that more can be prevented than currently achieved. Prevention thus is more important than ever.

Notes

1. The limiting factor is cost, rather than technological uncertainties. Energy required to capture and compress carbon dioxide increases the operating, investment, and capital costs of carbon capture and storage plants. In addition, fuel requirement of a carbon capture and storage plant is typically about 25 percent greater than that for a coal-fired plant, and about 15 percent than a gas-fired plant. Costs are also determined by the methods used in capturing and storing (through geological or other techniques).

2. This section draws from Neumayer, E., Plumper, T., and F. Barthel. 2014. The Political Economy of Natural Disaster Damage. *Global Environmental Change* 24 (1): 8–19

3. Ideally, disaster risk management must be anchored to an office with enough political authority to handle local governments and various development sectors. And even as decentralization is emphasized, a national policy is important to ensure coherence and a hospitable disaster risk investment environment.

4. The seven multilateral development banks in the study includes Asian Development Bank, African Development Bank, European Bank for Reconstruction and Development, European Investment Bank, Inter-American Development Bank, International Finance Corporation, and the World Bank.

7

A New Development
Paradigm

*This is the mega-development project of the world,
let's wake up and take advantage of it.*[1]
—Christiana Figueres, Executive Secretary of the United
Nations Framework Convention on Climate Change

Economists forecast the economic growth of countries and the global economy without taking into account needed climate investments nor the deleterious climate impacts. Short-term projections for 2015–2016 of growth rates of 3.5 percent for the global economy and 6 percent for Asia and the Pacific (IMF 2015; ADB 2015a) or various long-term projections of economic growth or other development attributes are cases in point.

But can the world sustain the projected types of growth and development without climate action? Can the world manage to address climate change and switch to a low-carbon economy in time?

Domestic reforms are paramount to any country's growth prospects. But cross-border factors matter too in a highly globalized world economy. Analogous to a global financial crisis, the danger of climate change threatens performance across countries. Climate-related disasters, that have crowded the headlines worldwide in recent years, are visible manifestations of this phenomenon. Floods and storms have been estimated to have inflicted sizable economic losses in recent years in Australia, the People's Republic of China, Indonesia, the Republic of Korea, Thailand, and Viet Nam, and the trend is set to worsen.

Multiple factors explain the mounting disasters: people's exposure to hazards, particularly in low-lying and coastal cities; greater vulnerability from soil erosion and deforestation; and just plain overcrowding. In addition, climate hazards are growing more menacing, which presents the most tangible reason to confront climate change. Scientists are cautious in linking any particular disaster to climate change. In the same way, economists are reluctant to pin higher inflation in any given month on rising money supply. But, as with inflation, the broader associations are unmistakable.

For some, the front and center needs of the poor will apparently heighten a dilemma balanced on growth versus the environment. But the dilemma presents a false choice. Relying on a longstanding growth pattern that fuels economic momentum with environmental destruction will only aggravate climate change. And it is the poor who stand to lose the most from the ravages of global warming. That is the clearest reason why climate action needs to be integral to the development strategy.

As Albert Einstein observed, "we cannot solve our problems with the same thinking we used when we created them." Economies must grow fast, but also need to grow differently. A strategy that values all three forms of capital—physical, human, and natural is needed. Sound growth policies have long been understood as those that expand investments in physical and human capital. But unless investment in natural capital is made, all bets are off. The United Nations' seventeen Sustainable Development Goals acknowledge this strong link between human well-being and environmental and ecosystem services.

In these circumstances, it is necessary to confront climate change systematically, as part of the growth paradigm. Even in the face of fluctuating oil prices, countries must commit to phasing out the use of fossil fuels, transition to a low-carbon economy and mitigate climate change. Governments also need to strengthen disaster resilience, improve natural resource use, and care for the urban environment; actions that help adapt to climate change.

The environment must be seen as integral in ensuring lasting economic growth. Investments are vital in physical and human capital, as well as in natural capital. International agreements on emissions can help underpin the value of the air we breathe. In addition to managing and safeguarding lands and seas, there is great significance to protecting the atmosphere. The air that the world shares and breathes presents the quintessential case of the global commons. Pricing and investments need to consider the spillover damages and the impacts not only on the present generation but the future ones as well.

Even with progress in international agreements in 2015, country actions remain paramount. Unilateral action can be undertaken vigorously, especially when local gains are clear. Cutting back on black carbon emissions, especially in polluted Beijing, New Delhi, and Manila, makes for cleaner air, boosting overall health. Increasing investments in solar photovoltaics (in the People's Republic of China and Japan), and in onshore wind (across Europe) should be taken as positive signals toward renewables. Accordingly, slashing fossil-fuel subsidies and establishing carbon taxes should be a top priority, and that requires confronting opposition from special and formidable interest groups.

Efforts to prevent natural disasters must be incorporated into national growth strategies. The mindset that regards natural disasters as one-off occurrences rather than a systemic problem must be transformed. Disaster risk management needs to be understood as an investment, going beyond relief and reconstruction to a dual approach of prevention and recovery. Japan invests some 5 percent of its national budget in DRR and has avoided much worse economic damage and deaths from disasters because of this (Government of Japan 2005).

High returns on preventive efforts are evident even where the total spending is far less. In the Philippines, the effects of flooding in Manila after heavy monsoon rains in August 2012 contrasted strongly with the devastation in the city from Tropical Storm Ketsana in 2009. The country has demonstrated payoffs from social media alerts, preemptive evacuations, and early warning systems. It also highlighted the benefits of the hazard maps and upgraded rain and water-level monitoring systems promoted by Project NOAH (the Nationwide Operational Assessment of Hazards).

Planners need to raise the priority for urban management and natural resource management. Urban agglomeration is associated with scale economies and productivity gains, but it is also a source of social costs. The five cities considered most vulnerable to natural hazards are all in Asia: Bangkok, Dhaka, Jakarta, Manila, and Yangon. These urban centers are overcrowded and situated in geographically fragile settings. Yet, fewer than 50 percent of Asians live in cities compared to 80 percent in Latin America, and further urbanization in Asia is inevitable. It is hard to overstate the priority for careful physical planning, environmental care, and judicious urban management.

Natural resource management gets short shrift in development programs, yet it is becoming a decisive factor in both the pace and quality of growth. Estimates of growth rates that take account of the destruction of natural capital are far less than those that do not. Sooner or later this divergence will impact traditional growth rates themselves. It is vital to accord greater emphasis for sustainable land use, sustainable agricultural practices, and forest and coastal management.

These steps help society adapt to the changing climate. The poor are hit harder by the effects of climate change than the rest of the population. Climate adaptation, including the building of resilient communities and peoples, as well as climate mitigation are essential parts of a poverty reduction strategy. Asia and the Pacific, which is the most at risk, must be in the front line of adaptation and also a powerful voice by switching to a low-carbon path and calling on others to do the same.

At the end of the day, a change in mindset on how growth is generated is needed. Traditional growth patterns at the expense of the environment will be self-defeating—a realization driven home by the stark reality of climate change. Economists can facilitate this understanding by building into their calculus the role of natural hazards and climate impacts in shaping lives and livelihoods.

Note

1. Christian Science Monitor. 2015. *UN Climate Chief: Global Warming Above 2 Degrees C is Not an Option.* http://www.csmonitor.com/Environment/ Energy/2015/1103/UN-climate-chief-Global-warming-above-2-degrees-C-is-not-an-option

Bibliography

ABS-CBN News. 2014. *A Tale of Three Disasters: The Wrath of Sendong, Pablo, and Yolanda.* http://www.abs-cbnnews.com/specials/3disasters.

Akerlof, G. 2014. "A Second Inconvenient Truth." *Finance and Development.* International Monetary Fund. September 2014, Vol. 51, No. 3. http://www.imf.org/external/pubs/ft/fandd/2014/09/nobels.htm.

Asian Development Bank (ADB). 2010. "Dealing with Disasters." *Development Asia,* January–March.

———. 2011. *Adapting to Climate Change: Strengthening the Climate Resilience of the Water Sector Infrastructure in Khulna, Bangladesh.* Manila: ADB.

———. 2012. *Key Indicators for Asia and the Pacific 2012: Green Urbanization in Asia.* Manila: ADB. http://www.adb.org/features/climate-change-asia-and-pacific- numbers.

———. 2014. ADB Statistical Database System. 1 September. Accessed July 7, 2015. https://sdbs.adb.org/sdbs/.

———. 2015a. *Asian Development Outlook 2015.* Manila: ADB.

———. 2015b. *Basic Statistics 2015.*

African Development Bank, Asian Development Bank, European Bank for Reconstruction and Development, European Investment Bank, Inter-American Development Bank, World Bank, and International Finance Corporation. 2013. Joint Report on MDB Climate Finance 2012. Joint Report.

American Council for an Energy-Efficient Economy (ACEEE). 2015. *Energy Efficiency Works: US Energy Use Per Dollar Cut in Half in Last 35 Years.* http://aceee.org/press/2015/06/energy-efficiency-works-us-energy.

Andersen, J. 2014. *5 Overlooked Deforestation Hotspots.* World Resources Institute. http://www.wri.org/blog/5-overlooked-deforestation-hotspots.

Anderson, J., and C. Bausch. 2006. *Climate Change and Natural Disasters: Scientific Evidence of a Possible Relation between Recent Natural Disasters and Climate Change.* Policy Brief for the EP Environment Committee (IP/A/ENVI/FWC/2005–35) Brief Number 02a/.

Angelsen, A., M. Brockhaus, W. D. Sunderlin, and L. Verchot, eds. 2012. *Analysing REDD+: Challenges and Choices.* Bogor: Center for International Forestry Research (CIFOR). doi:10.17528/cifor/003805.

AON Benfield. 2012. *2011 Thailand Floods Event Recap Report: Impact Forecasting.* March 2012. http://thoughtleadership.aonbenfield.com/Documents/20120314_impact_forecasting_thailand_flood_event_recap.pdf.

Arora, V., and A. Montenegro. 2011. "Small Temperature Benefits Provided by Realistic Afforestation Efforts." *Nature Geoscience* 4:514–18. doi:10.1038/ngeo1182.

Asian Disaster Preparedness Center. 2003. *The School Earthquake Safety Program in Kathmandu Valley. Safer Cities.* http://www.adpc.net/audmp/library/safer_cities/4.pdf.

Banerjee, A. 2006. Making Aid Work. *Boston Review*, 1 July. http://www.bostonreview.net/banerjee-making-aid-work.

Barasi, L. 2014. Have the Floods Finally Got Britain Worried about Climate Change? The *Carbon Brief – Blog*. 6 May. Accessed February 16, 2015. http://www.carbonbrief.org/blog/2014/05/have-the-floods-finally-got-britain-worried-about-climate-change/.

Baskin-Gerwitz, C. 2013. *The Rising Costs of Natural Disaster Insurance.* American Security Project. 7 October. https://www.americansecurityproject.org/the-rising-costs-of-natural-disaster-insurance/.

Bennett, J., W. Bertrand, C. Harkin, S. Samarasinghe, and H. Wickramatillake. 2006. *Coordination of International Humanitarian Assistance in Tsunami-Affected Countries.* London: Tsunami Evaluation Coalition.

Birkmann, J., N. Fernando, and N. Hettige. 2007. *Rapid Vulnerability Assessment in Sri Lanka.* Studies of the University: Research, Counsel, Education No. 7. Bonn: United Nations University, Institute for Environment and Human Security.

Bloomberg New Energy Finance. 2015a. *Global Trends in Clean Energy Investment.*

Bloomberg New Energy Finance. 9 January. http://about.bnef.com/presentations/clean-energy-investment-q4–2014-fact-pack/content/uploads/sites/4/2015/01/Q4-investment-fact-pack.pdf.

———. 2015b. *Wind and Solar Boost Cost Competitiveness versus Fossil Fuels.* http://about.bnef.com/press-releases/wind-solar-boost-cost-competitiveness-versus-fossil-fuels/.

Bohm, S., and S. Dabhi. 2009. "Upsetting the Offset: An Introduction." Chapter 1 in *Upsetting the Offset: The Political Economy of Carbon Markets.* Edited by Steffen Bohm and Siddhartha Dabhi, 360. London: MayflyBooks.

Bornstein, D. 2013. "Crowd Funding Clean Energy." *New York Times*, 3 March.

Bouwer, L. M. 2011. Have Disaster Losses Increased Due to Anthropogenic Climate Change? *Bulletin of the American Meteorological Society* 92:39–46.

Brooks, N., W. N. Adger, and P. M. Kelly. 2005. "The Determinants of Vulnerability and Adaptive Capacity at the National Level and the Implications for Adaptation." *Global Environmental Change* 15:151–63.

Buchner, B., M. Stadelmann, J. Wilkinson, F. Mazza, A. Rosenberg, and D. Abramskiehn. 2014. *Global Landscape of Climate Finance. Climate Policy Initiative.* http://climatepolicyinitiative.org/wp-content/uploads/2014/11/The-Global-Landscape-of-Climate-Finance-2014.pdf.

Carbon Disclosure Project. 2014. CDP Carbon Action. https://www.cdp.net/en-US/Programmes/Pages/Initiatives-CDP-Carbon-Action.aspx.

Carpenter, Z. 2013. Campaigning (and Winning) on Climate Change. *The Nation.* Blog. 6 November. http://www.thenation.com/blog/177039/virginia-climate-denial-losing-strategy#

Carrington, D. 2015. Indonesian forest fires on track to emit more CO_2 than UK. *The Guardian.* 7 October. http://www.theguardian.com/environment/2015/oct/07/indonesian-forest-fires-on-track-to-emit-more-co2-than-uk.

Center for Excellence in Disaster Management and Humanitarian Assistance (CFE-DMHA). 2015. Philippines: Disaster Management Reference Handbook. https://www.cfe-dmha.org/LinkClick.aspx?fileticket=fmpFiMdOl_g%3d&portalid=0.

Center for International Forest Research (CIFOR). 2015. *Clearing the Smoke: The Causes and Consequences of Indonesian Forest Fires.* 30 October. Retrieved from Center for International Forest Research: http://blog.cifor.org/37016/clearing-the-smoke-the-causes-and-consequences-of-indonesias-fires?fnl=en.

Chen, Y., Ebenstein, A., Greenstone, M., and H. Li. 2013. *Evidence on the Impact of Sustained Exposure to Air Pollution on Life Expectancy from the People's Republic of China's Huai River Policy.* Proceedings of the National Academy of Sciences of the United States of America. July 8. doi:10.1073/pnas.1300018110.

Christian Science Monitor. 2015. UN Climate Chief: Global Warming Above 2 Degrees C is Not an Option. http://www.csmonitor.com/Environment/Energy/2015/1103/UN-climate-chief-Global-warming-above-2-degrees-C-is-not-an-option.

Coady, D., Parry, I.W.H., Sears, L., and B. Shang. 2015. *How Large are Global Energy Subsidies?* IMF Working Paper WP/15/105. Washington, DC: International Monetary Fund.

Comiso, J. C., G. P. Perez, and L. V. Stock. 2015. "Enhanced Pacific Ocean Sea Surface Temperature and Its Relation to Typhoon Haiyan." *Journal of Environmental Science and Management* 18 (1): 1–10. Retrieved from http://journals.uplb.edu.ph/index.php/JESAM/article/view/1282/pdf_23.

Cook, J., D. Nuccitelli, S. A. Green, M. Richardson, B. Winkler, R. Painting, R. Way, P. Jacobs, and A. Skuce. 2013. "Quantifying the Consensus on Anthropogenic Global Warming in the Scientific Literature." *Environmental Research Letters* 8 (2). doi:10.1088/1748-9326/8/2/024024.

Coumou, D., and S. Rahmstorf. 2012. "A Decade of Weather Extremes." *Nature Climate Change* 2:491–96. doi:10.1038/nclimate1452.

Creuheras, S. 2015. *Energy Efficiency: A Field of Opportunity for the G20.* Sustainable International Institute for Sustainable Development. http://energy-l.iisd.org/guest-articles/energy-efficiency-a-field-of-opportunity-for-the-g20/.

Darwanto, H. 2012. *Preliminary Examination of Existing Methodologies for Allocating and Tracking National Government Budget for Disaster Risk Reduction in Indonesia.* United Nations International Strategy for Disaster Reduction. http://www.unisdr.org/files/32377_32377indonesiadraftdrrinvestmenttra.pdf.

Dilley, M., R. S. Chen, U. Deichmann, A. L. Lerner-Lam, M. Arnold, J. Agwe, P. Buys, O. Kjekstad, B. Lyon, and G. Yetman. 2005. *Natural Disaster Hotspots: A Global Risk Analysis. Disaster Management Series No.5.* Washington, DC: World Bank/IBRD and Columbia University.

Disaster Resilience Leadership Academy (DRLA). 2011. *Haiti Humanitarian Aid Evaluation: Structured Analysis Summary Report.* Disaster Resilience Leadership Academy: New Orleans. http://www.drlatulane.org/groups/haiti-humanitarian-aid-evaluation.

Donato, D. C., J. B. Kauffman, D. Murdiyarso, S. Kurnianto, M. Stidham, and M. Kanninen. 2011. "Mangroves among the Most Carbon-Rich Forest in the Tropics." *Nature Geoscience* 4:293–97. doi:10.1038/ngeo1123.

EM-DAT/UNISDR. 2011. *Disasters in Numbers. Prevention Web.* http://www.preventionweb.net/files/24697_246922011disasterstats1.pdf.

EM-DAT/UNISDR. 2012. Disasters in Numbers. Prevention Web. http://www.preventionweb.net/files/31685_factsheet2012.pdf.

EM-DAT/UNISDR. 2013. Disasters in Numbers. CRED. http://www.cred.be/sites/ default/files/Disasters-in-numbers-2013.pdf.

EM-DAT: The OFDA/CRED International Disaster Database. Université Catholique de Louvain. Brussels, Belgium. www.emdat.be.

Emanuel, K. 2005. "Increasing Destructiveness of Tropical Cyclones over the Past 30 Years." *Nature* 436:686–88. doi:10.1038/nature03906.

European Bank for Reconstruction and Development. 2011. *The Low Carbon Transition. Special Report on Climate Change.* London: European Bank for Reconstruction and Development.

Evaluation Cooperation Group. 2010. *Ensuring Biodiversity in a Sustainable Future: Lessons from Evaluations.* ECG Briefing Note, 13 October.

Federal Ministry for the Environment, Nature Conservation, Building and Nuclear Safety (BMUB). 2015. *Climate Action in Figures.* Berlin: BMUB.

Fermino, J. 2013. "Bloomberg Rolls Out $20 Billion Plan to Protect City from Natural Disasters." *New York Daily News*, 11 June.

Frankfurt School-UNEP Collaborating Centre for Climate and Sustainable Energy Finance and Bloomberg New Energy Finance. 2015. Global Trends in Renewable Energy Investment 2015. http://fs-unep-centre.org/publications/global-trends-renewable-energy-investment-2015.

Freeman III, C. W., and A. Searight. 2010. "The Politics of Climate Change in Asia." In *Asia's Response to Climate Change and Natural Disasters: Implications for an Evolving Regional Architecture – A Report of the CSIS Asian Regionalism Initiative*, edited by R. S. Wang and J. D. Bean, 132. Washington, DC: Center for Strategic and International Studies.

Friedman, T. 2013. It's Lose-Lose Vs Win-Win-Win-Win-Win. *New York Times*, 17 March. http://www.nytimes.com/2013/03/17/opinion/sunday/friedman-its-lose-lose-vs-win-win-win-win-win.html?pagewanted=all.

Furman, J., R. Shadbegian, and J. Stock. 2015. The Cost of Delaying Action to Stem Climate Change: A Meta-Analysis. VOX CEPR's Policy Portal. 25 February. http://www.voxeu.org/article/cost-delaying-action-stem-climate-change-meta-analysis.

Füssel, H. -M., and R. J. T. Klein. 2006. "Climate Change Vulnerability Assessments: An Evolution of Conceptual Thinking." *Climatic Change* 75 (3): 301–29.

Giddens, A. 2009. *The Politics of Climate Change.* Cambridge: Polity Press.

Global Commission on the Economy and Climate. 2014. The New Climate Economy Report: Better Growth, Better Climate. Retrieved from http://newclimateeconomy.report/.

———. 2015. *The 2015 New Climate Economy Report: Seizing the Global Opportunity.* http://newclimateeconomy.report/.

Global Facility for Disaster Risk Reduction and Recovery (GFDRR). n.d. Stories of Impact: Strengthening Urban Resilience in Bangladesh. https://www.gfdrr.org/sites/default/files/publication/Bangladesh.pdf.

Gonzalez D., M. Verónica, D. Verner, M. E. Corrales, J. M. Puerta, M. P. Mendieta Umaña, C. Morales, D. Suarez, A. M. Linares, L. Scholl, O. Quintanilla, M. Celse L'Hoste, L. Alvarez Prado, A. Molina, R. Marto, J. H. Christensen, M. Ashwill, C. Diewald, R. Schneider, J. Lisansky, J. Uquillas, and J. Redwood. 2014. *Climate Change at the IDB: Building Resilience and Reducing Emissions.* Washington DC: Inter-American Development Bank. https://publications.iadb.org/handle/11319/6692?locale-attribute=en#sthash.aoE317hK.dpuf.

Government of Japan. 2005. National Report of Japan on Disaster Reduction. World Conference on Disaster Reduction. http://www.unisdr.org/2005/mdgs-drr/national-reports/Japan-report.pdf.

Government of the Philippines-GFDRR. 2009. Philippines: Typhoons Ondoy and Pepeng. Post-Disaster Needs Assessment: Main Report, GFDRR.

Greenstone, M., J. Nilekani, R. Pande, N. Ryan, A. Sudarshan, and A. Sugathan. 2015. "Lower Pollution, Longer Lives: Life Expectancy Gains if India Reduced Particulate Matter Pollution." *Economic and Political Weekly* 50 (8): 40–46.

Grinsted, A., J. C. Moore, and S. Jevrejeva. 2013. "Projected Atlantic Hurricane Surge Threat from Rising Temperatures." *Proceedings of the National Academy of Sciences.* http://www.pnas.org/cgi/doi/10.1073/pnas.1209980110.

Guha-Sapir, D., R. Below, and Ph. Hoyois–EM-DAT. 2012. *The CRED/OFDA International Disaster Database.* Brussels: Université Catholique de Louvain. Accessed February 16, 2015. http://www.emdat.be.

Guha-Sapir, D., F. Vos, R. Below, and S. Ponserre. 2012. *Annual Disaster Statistical Review 2011: The Numbers and Trends.* Brussels: Centre for Research on the Epidemiology of Disasters.

Haddow, G., and J. Bullock. 2003. *The Future of Emergency Management.* Washington, DC: Institute for Crisis, Disaster and Risk Management.

Hallegatte, S. 2011. How economic growth and rational decisions can make disaster losses grow faster than wealth. Policy Research Working Paper 5617. World Bank.

———. 2012. "Economics: The Rising Costs of Hurricanes." *Nature Climate Change* 2:148–9. doi:10.1038/nclimate1427.

Hallegatte, S., C. Green, R. J. Nicholls, and J. Corfee-Morlot. 2013. "Future Flood Losses in Major Coastal Cities." *Nature Climate Change* 3:802–6.

———. 2016. *Shock Waves: Managing the Impacts of Climate Change on Poverty.* Climate Change and Development Series. Washington, DC: World Bank. doi:10.1596/978-1-4648-0673-5. License: Creative Commons Attribution CC BY 3.0 IGO.

Handrich, L., C. Kemfert, A. Mattes, F. Pavel, and T. Traber. 2015. *Turning Point: Decoupling Greenhouse Gas Emissions from Economic Growth.* Berlin: Heinrich Böll Stiftung.

Hansen, M. C. 2013. Hansen/UMD/Google/USGS/NASA Tree Cover Loss and Gain Area. University of Maryland, Google, USGS, and NASA. http://www.globalforestwatch.org (accessed through Global Forest Watch on 29 July 2015).

Hansen, M. C., P. V. Potapov, R. Moore, S. A. Hancher, M. Turubanova, A. Tyukavina, D. Thau, S. V. Stehman, S. J. Goetz, T. R. Loveland, A. Kommareddy, A. Egorov, L. Chini, C. O. Justice, and J. R. G. Townshend. 2013. "High-Resolution Global Maps of 21st-Century Forest Cover Change." *Science* 342 (6160): 850–3. doi:10.1126/science.1244693.

Harris, N., S. Minnemeyer, F. Stolle, and O. A. Payne. 2015. *Indonesia's Fire Outbreaks Producing More Daily Emissions than Entire US Economy.* 16 October. Retrieved from World Resources Institute: http://www.wri.org/blog/2015/10/indonesia%E2%80%99s-fire-outbreaks-producing-more-daily-emissions-entire-us-economy.

Harvey, F. 2014. "Climate Change Report: Prevent Damage by Overhauling Global Economy." *The Guardian,* 16 September. http://www.theguardian.com/environment/2014/sep/16/climate-change-report-damage-overhaul-global- economy.

Heal, G. 2008. Climate Economics: A Meta-Review and Some Suggestions. Working Paper 13927. National Bureau of Economic Research.

Hoerling, M., J. Eischeid, J. Perlwitz, X. Quan, T. Zhang, and P. Pegion. 2012. "On the Increased Frequency of Mediterranean Drought." *Journal of Climate* 25:2146–61.

Hosonuma, N., M. Herold, V. De Sy, R. S. De Fries, M. Brockhaus, L. Verchot, A. Angelsen, and E. Romijn. 2012. "An Assessment of Deforestation and Forest Degradation Drivers in Developing Countries." *Environmental Research Letters* 7 (4). doi:10.1088/1748–9326/7/4/044009.

Independent Evaluation Department (IED). 2012. *ADB's Response to Natural Disasters and Risks. Special Evaluation Study.* Manila: ADB.

———. 2013. *The Rise of Natural Disasters in Asia and the Pacific: Learning from ADB's Experience.* Manila: ADB.

———. 2015. *Annual Evaluation Review 2015.* Manila: ADB.

Internal Displacement Monitoring Centre (IDMC). 2015. Philippines IDP Figures *Analysis.* http://www.internal-displacement.org/south-and-south-east-asia/philippines/figures-analysis.

International Energy Agency (IEA). 2014. *World Energy Outlook.* http://www.worldenergyoutlook.org/resources/energysubsidies/.

———. 2015. *Energy and Climate Change: World Energy Outlook Special Briefing for COP21*. Paris: IEA.

International Federation of Red Cross and Red Crescent Societies (IFRC). 2005. South Asia Earthquake Tragedy and Destruction in Kashmir. *The Magazine of International Federation of Red Cross and Red Crescent Societies*. http://www.redcross.int/EN/mag/magazine2005_3/4–9.html.

———. 2013a. Typhoon Bopha – Case study: Pablo E. Villafane and Gibertz V. Luas. 11 January. http://www.ifrc.org/en/news-and-media/news-stories/asia-pacific/philippines/typhoon-bopha---case-study-pablo-e-villafane-and-gibertz-v-luas-60548/#sthash.rOSq85tD.dpuf.

———. 2013b. World Disaster Report. http://www.ifrc.org/publications-and-reports/world-disasters-report/.

International Monetary Fund (IMF). 2015. *World Economic Outlook 2015*. April. Washington, DC: IMF. http://www.imf.org/external/pubs/ft/weo/2015/01/.

Intergovernmental Panel on Climate Change (IPCC). 2012a. "Glossary of Terms." In *Managing the Risks of Extreme Events and Disasters to Advance Climate Change Adaptation*. A Special Report of Working Groups I and II of the IPCC, edited by , C. B. Field, V. Barros, T. F. Stocker, Q. Dahe, D. J. Dokken, K. L. Ebi, M. D. Mastrandrea, K. J. Mach, G. -K. Plattner, S. K. Allen, M. Tignor, and P. M. Midgley, 555–64. Cambridge and New York: Cambridge University Press.

———. 2012b. "Summary for Policymakers." In *Managing the Risks of Extreme Events and Disasters to Advance Climate Change Adaptation*. A Special Report of Working Groups I and II of the Intergovernmental Panel on Climate Change, edited byC. B. Field, V. Barros, T. F. Stocker, Q. Dahe, D. J. Dokken, K. L. Ebi, M. D. Mastrandrea, K. J. Mach, G. -K. Plattner, S. K. Allen, M. Tignor, and P. M. Midgley, 1–19. Cambridge and New York: Cambridge University Press.

———. 2013. "Summary for Policymakers." In *Climate Change 2013: The Physical Science Basis. Contribution of Working Group I to the Fifth Assessment Report of the Intergovernmental Panel on Climate Change*, edited by T. F. Stocker, D. Qin, G. -K. Plattner, M. Tignor, S. K. Allen, J. Boschung, A. Nauels, Y. Xia, V. Bex, and P. M. Midgley.. Cambridge and New York: Cambridge University Press.

———. 2014a. "Summary for Policymakers." In *Climate Change 2014: Impacts, Adaptation, and Vulnerability. Part A: Global and Sectoral Aspects. Contribution of Working Group II to the Fifth Assessment Report of the Intergovernmental Panel on Climate Change*, edited byC. B. Field, V. R. Barros, D. J. Dokken, K. J. Mach, M. D. Mastrandrea, T. E. Bilir, M. Chatterjee, K. L. Ebi, Y. O. Estrada, R. C. Genova, B. Girma, E. S. Kissel, A. N. Levy, S. MacCracken, P. R. Mastrandrea, and L. L. White, 1–32. Cambridge and New York: Cambridge University Press.

———. 2014b. "Summary for Policymakers." In *Climate Change 2014: Mitigation of Climate Change. Contribution of Working Group III to the Fifth Assessment Report of the Intergovernmental Panel on Climate Change*, edited by Edenhofer, O., Pichs-Madruga, R., Sokona, Y., Minx, J.C., Farahani, E., Kadner, S., Seyboth, K., Adler, A., Baum, I., Brunner, S., Eickemeier, P., Kriemann, B., Savolainen, J., Schlomer, S., von Stechow, C., and T. Zwickel. Cambridge and New York: Cambridge University Press.

———. 2014c. *Climate Change 2014: Synthesis Report. Contribution of Working Groups I, II and III to the Fifth Assessment Report of the Intergovernmental Panel on Climate Change* (Core Writing Team, Pachauri, R. K., and L. A. Meyer. ed). IPCC, Geneva, Switzerland, 151 pp.

Jack, A. 2014. "Financial Times Special Report: Urban Resilience." *Financial Times.* 7 April.

Japan Meteorological Agency. 2014. Climate Change Monitoring Report 2013. http://www.jma.go.jp/jma/en/NMHS/indexe_ccmr.html.

Japan Today. 2015. *Experts Split Over Nuclear Power as Panacea for Climate Change.* 6 December. http://www.japantoday.com/category/opinions/view/experts-split-over-nuclear-power-as-panacea-for-climate-change.

Jenkins, J. 2014. When Politics Constraints Carbon Pricing, Part 2: 6 Tips for Improving Climate Change Policy. *The Energy Collective – Columns.* 24 July. http://theenergycollective.com/jessejenkins/442661/politics-and-climate-policy-part-2-how-improve-politically-constrained-carbon-pr.

Kahn, M. E. 2005. "The Death Toll from Natural Disasters: The Role of Income, Geography, and Institutions." *The Review of Economics and Statistics* 872:271–84.

Keeling, R. 2015. Scripps Institution of Oceanography. January. Accessed February 19, 2105. http://www.scrippsco2.ucsd.edu/.

Kellenberg, D. K., and A. M. Mobarak. 2008. "Does Rising Income Increase or Decrease Damage Risk from Natural Disasters?" *Journal of Urban Economics* 63 (3): 788–802.

Kellet, J., and A. Caravani. 2013. *Financing Disaster Risk Reduction: A Twenty Year Story of International Aid.* Global Facility for Disaster Reduction and Recovery and Overseas Development Institute. http://www.odi.org/sites/odi.org.uk/files/odi-assets/publications-opinion-files/8574.pdf.

Kellet, J., and D. Sparks. 2012. *Disaster Risk Reduction: Spending Where it Should Count.* Wells: Global Humanitarian Assistance.

Kelman, I. 2013. *Disaster Mitigation is Cost Effective.* World Development Report 2014 Background Note. Washington, DC: The World Bank.

Kemper, A, and R Martin. 2013. "Climate Talks Will Fail Unless Parties Agree to a Carbon Price." *The Guardian,* 25 November.

Kim, C. K. 2010. "The Effects of Natural Disasters on Long-Run Economic Growth." *The Michigan Journal of Business* 41:15–49.

Kingsnorth, P. 2014. "The Four Degrees." *London Review of Books* 36 (20): 17–18.

Knutson, T. R., J. L. McBride, J. Chan, K. Emanuel, G. Holland, C. Landsea, I. Held, J. P. Kossin, A. K. Srivastava, and M. Sugi. 2010. "Tropical Cyclones and Climate Change." *Nature Geoscience* 3:157–63.

Kreft, S., D. Eckstein, L. Junghans, C. Kerestan, and U. Hagen . 2014. *Global Climate Risk Index 2015.* Germanwatch.

Kunkel, K. E., T. R. Karl, H. Brooks, J. Kossin, J. H. Lawrimore, D. Arndt, L. Bosart, D. Changnon, S. L. Cutter, N. Doesken, K. Emanuel, P. Y. Groisman,

R. W. Katz, T. Knutson, J. O'brien, C. J. Paciorek, T. C. Peterson, K. Redmond, D. Robinson, J. Trapp, R. Vose, S. Weaver, M. Wehner, K. Wolter, and D. Wuebbles. 2013. "Monitoring and Understanding Trends in Extreme Storms: State of Knowledge." *Bulletin of the American Meteorological Society* 94 (4): 499–514. doi:http://dx.doi.org/10.1175/BAMS-D-11-00262.1.

Lamb, K. 2015. "Indonesia's Fires Labelled a 'Crime against Humanity' as 500,000 Suffer." *The Guardian*. 26 October.

Lang, C. 2009. *20% of CO_2 Emissions from Deforestation? Make that 12%.* 4 November. http://www.redd-monitor.org/2009/11/04/20-of-co2-emissions-from-deforestation-make-that-12/.

Lee, M., D. Park, and H. Saunders. 2014. *Asia's Energy Adequacy, Environmental Sustainability, and Affordability: An Overview.* ADB Economics Working Paper Series No. 398. http://www.adb.org/sites/default/files/publication/42605/ewp-398.pdf.

Lenderink, G., and E. van Meijgaard. 2008. "Increase in Hourly Precipitation Extreme beyond Expectations from Temperature Changes." *Nature Geoscience* 1:511–14. doi:10.1038/ngeo262.

Llyod-Jones, T. 2006. Mind the Gap! Post-disaster reconstruction and the transition from humanitarian relief. RICS/University of Westminster.

London School of Economics and Political Science/Grantham Research Institute on Climate Change and the Environment (LSE/GRI). 2015. 2015 Global Climate Legislation Study at a Glance. http://www.lse.ac.uk/GranthamInstitute/legislation/2015-global-climate-legislation-study-at-a-glance/.

Mackey, B., C. Prentice, W. Steffen, J. I. House, D. Lindenmayer, H. Keith, and S. Berry. 2013. "Untangling the Confusion around Land Carbon Science and Climate Change Mitigation Policy." *Nature Climate Change* 3:552–57. doi:10.1038/nclimate1804.

Maplecroft. 2014. *Climate Change and Environmental Risk Atlas 2015.* http://www.maplecroft.com.

Matthews, J. 2014. "Renewables Will Go from Strength to Strength." *Financial Times*, 21 December.

McElroy, A. 2013. *News Archive: Evacuation Saves Whole Island from Typhoon Haiyan.* United Nations International Strategy for Disaster Reduction. http://www.unisdr.org/archive/35524.

McKibben, B. 2014. "Climate: Will We Lose the Endgame." *New York Review of Books*, 10 July.

Mendelsohn, R. 2009. *Climate Change and Economic Growth.* Working Paper No. 60. Commission on Growth and Development. Washington, DC. https://environment.yale.edu/files/biblio/YaleFES-00000397.pdf.

Mendelsohn, R., K. Emanuel, S. Chonabayashi, and L. Bakkensen. 2012. "The Impact of Climate Change on Global Tropical Cyclone Damage." *Nature Climate Change* 2: 205–9. doi:10.1038/nclimate1357.

Min, S. K., X. Zhang, F. W. Zwiers, and G. C. Hegerl. 2011. "Human Contribution to More Intense Precipitation Extremes." *Nature* 470 (7334): 378–81. doi:10.1038/nature09763.

Mohleji, S., and P. Jr. Roger. 2014. "Reconciliation of Trends in Global and Regional Economic Losses from Weather Events: 1980–2008." *Natural*

Hazards Review 15 (4): 04014009. doi:http://dx.doi.org/10.1061/(ASCE) NH.1527–6996.0000141.

Morris, Craig, and Pehnt, Martin. 2015 revision. *The German Energiewende (Energy Transition)*. Berlin: Heinrich Böll Foundation. www.energytransition.de.

Mukhim, Patricia. 2014. "Floods in the North-East: Lack of Planning and Red Tape." *Economic and Political Weekly*, 14 October.

Munich Re. 2012. *Natural Catastrophes in 2011*. http://www.munichre. com/site/mram-mobile/get/documents_E-564631040/mram/assetpool. mr_america/PDFs/4_Events/2011_Overview_World.pdf.

———. 2014. *Loss Events Worldwide 2013*. https://www.munichre.com/ site/touch-naturalhazards/get/documents_E792052670/mr/assetpool. shared/Documents/5_Touch/Natural%20Hazards/NatCatService/ Annual%20Statistics/2013/MunichRe-Natcatservice-Naturaldisaster2013- Ordered-by-Ins.pdf.

———. 2015. Loss Events Worldwide 1980–2014. https://www.munichre. com/site/touch-naturalhazards/get/documents_E-567437233/mr/asset- pool.shared/Documents/5_Touch/_NatCatService/Significant-Natural- Catastrophes/2014/10-costliest-events-ordered-by-overall-losses.pdf.

Nakhooda, Smita. 2008. *Correcting the World's Greatest Market Failure: Climate Change and the Multilateral Development Banks*. WRI Issue Brief. World Resources Institute. Washington, DC, June. http://www. wri.org/sites/default/files/pdf/correcting_the_worlds_greatest_market_ failure.pdf.

NASA Earth Observatory. 2015. *Smoke Blankets Indonesia*. Retrieved from NASA Earth Observatory. http://earthobservatory.nasa.gov/IOTD/view. php?id=86681&eocn=image&eoci=related_image.

NASA GISS. 2015. *GISS Surface Temperature Analysis (GISTEMP)*. 16 January. Accessed February 2, 2015. http://data.giss.nasa.gov/gistemp/.

National Economic and Development Authority. 2013. *Reconstruction Assistance on Yolanda*. Pasig City: National Economic and Development Authority.

National Oceanic and Atmospheric Administration (NOAA) AOML Hurri- cane Research Division. Frequently Asked Questions. Accessed June 24, 2015. http://www.aoml.noaa.gov/hrd/tcfaq/tcfaqHED.html.

Neumayer, E., and F. Barthel. 2010. "Normalizing Economic Loss from Natural Disasters: A Global Analysis." *Global Environmental Change* 21 (1): 13–24.

Neumayer, E., Plumper, T., and F. Barthel. 2014. "The Political Economy of Natural Disaster Damage." *Global Environmental Change* 24 (1): 8–19.

NOAA National Centers for Environmental Information. 2010. "State of the Climate: Global Hazards for August 2010." September. http://www.ncdc. noaa.gov/sotc/hazards/201008.

———. 2015. "State of the Climate: Global Analysis for November 2015." December. Accessed December 28, 2015. https://www.ncdc.noaa.gov/ sotc/global/201507.

NOAA National Climatic Data Center. 2015. "State of the Climate: Global Analysis for Annual 2014." January. Accessed June 11, 205. http://www. ncdc.noaa.gov/sotc/global/201413.

NOAA National Weather Service. JetStream-Online School for Weather. 7 April. Accessed June 24, 2015. http://www.srh.noaa.gov/jetstream/ tropics/tc_basins.htm.

Noy, I. 2008. "The Macroeconomic Consequences of Disasters." *Journal of Development Economics* 88:221–31.

Nuccitelli, D. 2014. "California Just Had Its Worst Drought in Over 1200 Years, As Temperatures and Risks Rise." *The Guardian*, 8 December. http://www.theguardian.com/environment/climate-consensus-97-per-cent/2014/dec/08/california-just-had-its-worst-drought-in-over-1200-years.

———. 2015. Climate finance in 2013–14 and the USD 100 billion goal. A report by the Organisation for Economic Co-operation and Development (OECD) in collaboration with Climate Policy Initiative (CPI). http://www.oecd.org/environment/cc/OECD-CPI-Climate-Finance-Report.htm.

OECD and International Energy Agency (IEA). 2014. *Energy Efficiency Market Report 2014*. http://www.oecd-ilibrary.org/energy/energy-efficiency-market-report- 2014_9789264218260-en.

Office of the Press Secretary. 2014. FACT SHEET: U.S.-The People's Republic of China Joint Announcement on Climate Change and Clean Energy Cooperation. The White House. 11 November. Accessed July 10, 2015. https://www.whitehouse.gov/the-press-office/2014/11/11/fact-sheet-us-the People's Republic of China-joint-announcement-climate-change-and-clean-energy-c.

Okuyama, Y., and S. Sahin. 2009. Impact Estimation of Disasters: A Global Aggregate for 1960 to 2007. Policy Research Working Paper 4963. World Bank, GFDRR and International University of Japan.

Oreskes, N. 2004. "The Scientific Consensus on Climate Change." *Science* 306 (5702):1686.

OXFAM. 2014. The Right Move? Ensuring Durable Relocation after Typhoon Haiyan. OXFAM Briefing Paper, OXFAM International.

Pacheco, P., M. Aguilar-Støen, J. Börner, A. Etter, L. Putzel, and M. del Carmen Vera Diaz. 2011. "Landscape Transformation in Tropical Latin America: Assessing Trends and Policy Implications for REDD+." *Forests* 2 (1): 1–29. doi:10.3390/f2010001.

Padgett, T. 2010. "Chile and Haiti: A Tale of Two Earthquakes." *Time*. 1 March. http://content.time.com/time/world/article/0,8599,1968576,00.html.

Page, S. E., F. Siegert, J. O. Rieley, H. -D. V. Boehm, A. Jaya, and S. Limin. 2002. "The Amount of Carbon Released from Peat and Forest Fires in Indonesia in 1997." *Nature* 20: 61–64.

Philippine Atmospheric, Geophysical and Astronomical Services Administration (PAGASA). n.d. Climate Change in the Philippines. PAGASA. http://www.pagasa.dost.gov.ph/index.php/climate-change-in-the-philippines (accessed 17 February 2015).

Pall, P., T. Aina, D. A. Stone, P. A. Stott, T. Nozawa, A. G. J. Hilberts, D. Lohmann, and M. R. Allen. 2011. "Anthropogenic Greenhouse Gas Contribution to Flood Risk in England and Wales in Autumn 2000." *Nature* 470:382–85.

Parenti, C. 2013. "A Radical Approach to the Climate Crisis." *Dissent Magazine*. Summer. http://www.dissentmagazine.org/article/a-radical-approach-to-the-climate-crisis.

Petri, P., and V. Thomas. 2013. *Development Imperatives for the Asian Century*. ADB Working Paper Series No. 360. Manila: Asian Development Bank.

Philippine Statistics Authority. 2013. Poverty Statistics-Data and Charts. Accessed July 27, 2015. http://www.nscb.gov.ph/poverty/dataCharts.asp.

Phillips, D. 2014. "Report Suggests Forest-Cutting Can immediately Harm Climatic Patterns." *Washington Post*, 19 December. http://www.washingtonpost.com/world/report-suggests-forest-cutting-can-have-an-immediate-effect-on-climate/2014/12/18/ba392600–86f6–11e4-abcf-5a3d7b3b20b8_story.html? utm_source=Feb%2FMarch+2015+The+REDD%2B+Resource&utm_campaign=Feb-March+2015+UN-REDD+news.

Pindyck, R. 2013. "Climate Change Policy: What Do the Models Tell Us?" *Journal of Economic Literature* 51 (3): 860–72.

Porrura, M. E., E. Corbera, and K. Brown. 2007. *Reducing Greenhouse Gas Emissions from Deforestation in Developing Countries: Revisiting Assumptions*. Working Paper 115. Tyndall Centre for Climate Change Research. http://www.tyndall.ac.uk/sites/default/files/wp115.pdf.

Porter, E. 2013. "A Model for Reducing Emissions." *New York Times*, 13 March.

Prasad, P. 1976. "Poverty and Bondage." *Economic and Political Weekly* XI(31):1269–1272.

Prevention Web. 2015a. India's Heatwave a Lesson for Sendai Framework. 12 June. http://www.preventionweb.net/english/professional/news/v.php?id=44814.

———. 2015b. Vanuatu: Disaster Preparedness Saved Lives—UNDP. 26 May. http://www.preventionweb.net/english/professional/news/v.php?id=44535&utm_source=pw_search&utm_medium=search&utm_campaign=search.

Rahmstorf, S., and D. Coumou. 2011. "Increase of Extreme Events in a Warming World." *Proceedings of the National Academy of Sciences of the United States of America* 108 (44): 17905–9.

Rentschler, J. E. 2013. *Why Resilience Matters: The Poverty Impacts of Disasters*. World Bank Policy Research Working Paper No. 6699. Washington, DC: World Bank.

Responding to Climate Change (RTCC). 2015. Kyoto Protocol: 10 Years of the World's First Climate Change Treaty. February 16. http://www.rtcc.org/2015/02/16/kyoto-protocol-10-years-of-the-worlds-first-climate-change-treaty/.

Ruddell, S., R. Sampson, M. Smith, R. Giffen, J. Cathcart, J. Hagan, D. Sosland, J. Godbee, J. Heissenbuttel, S. Lovett, J. Helms, W. Price, and R. Simpson. 2007. "The Role for Sustainable Managed Forests in Climate Change Mitigation." *Journal of Forestry* 105 (6): 314–19. http://michigansaf.org/ForestInfo/Ruddell-EtAl-2007.pdf.

Sachs, J. 2014. "Breaking Down the Barriers in Negotiations on Climate Change." *Taipei Times*, 28 June.

Schaffer, T. 2010. "Asian Regional Institutions and Climate Change." In *Asia's Response to Climate Change and Natural Disasters: Implications for an Evolving Regional Architecture – A Report of the CSIS Asian Regionalism Initiative*, no. 132, edited by C. W. Freeman III, M. J. Green, Wang, R. S., and J. D. Bea. Washington, DC: Center for Strategic and International Studies.

Schreider, S. Y., D. I. Smith, and A. J. Jakeman. 2000. "Climate Change Impacts on Urban Flooding." *Climatic Change* 47 (1–2): 91–115.

Shah, J. 2016. "Test Your Knowledge on Renewable Energy." Asian Development Blog. 31 March 2016. http://blogs.adb.org/blog/test-your-knowledge-renewable-energy.

Skidmore, M., and H. Toya. 2002. "Do Natural Disasters Promote Long-Run Growth?" *Economic Inquiry* 40 (4): 664–87.

Stern, N. 2006. Stern Review: The Economics of Climate Change. UK Government Web Archive. http://webarchive.nationalarchives.gov. uk/20100407172811/,http://www.hm-treasury.gov.uk/stern_review_report.htm.

Stern, N. 2007. The Economics of Climate Change, Second IG Patel Lecture. New Delhi, 26 October.

———. 2013a. *Ethics, Equity and the Economics of Climate Change. Paper 1: Science and Philosophy*. Working Paper. Leeds and London: Centre for Climate Change Economics and Policy.

———. 2013b. "The Structure of Economic Modeling of the Potential Impacts of Climate Change: Grafting Gross Underestimation of Risk onto Already Narrow Science Models." *Journal of Economic Literature* 51 (3): 838–59.

Stern, N., and I. Noble. 2008. "Achieving Low-Carbon Growth for the World." *Development Outreach* 10 (World Bank). https://openknowledge.worldbank. org/handle/10986/4525.

Stiglitz, J. E. 2013. The Post-Crisis Crises. 7 January. Project Syndicate. https:// www.project-syndicate.org/commentary/global-warming--inequality--and-structural-change-by-joseph-e--stiglitz?barrier=true.

Stott, P. A., D. A. Stone, and M. R. Allen. 2004. "Human Contribution to the European Heatwave of 2003." *Nature* 432:610–14.

Straatsma, M., J. Ettema, and B. Krol. 2010. Flooding and Pakistan: Casuses, Impact and Risk Assessment. *ITC Faculty of Geo-Information Science and Earth Observation of the Universaity of Twente*. October. http://www.itc. nl/flooding-and-pakistan.

Strauss, C. n.d. When to Give: The Four Phases of Disaster Relief. *Fidelity Charitable*. Accessed August 26, 2015. http://www.fidelitycharitable.org/ giving-strategies/disaster-relief/disaster-relief.shtml.

Sturgis, L. A., T. C. Smythe, and A. E. Tucci. 2014. Port Recovery in the Aftermath of Hurricane Sandy: Improving Port Resiliency in the Era of Climate Change. Center for a New American Security. http://www. cnas.org/sites/default/files/publications-pdf/CNAS_HurricaneSandy_VoicesFromTheField.pdf.

Sun-Star. 2013. *No Longer Typhoon Free.* 31 August, http://archive.sunstar. com.ph/weekend-davao/2013/08/31/no-longer-typhoon-free-300760.

Tanner, T., T. Mitchell, E. Polack, and B. Guenther. 2009. *Urban Governance for Adaptation: Assessing Climate Change Resilience in Ten Asian Cities.* IDS Working Paper 315. Institute of Development Studies.

Tans, P. 2015. NOAA/ESRL. 6 January. Accessed February 19, 2015. www.esrl. noaa.gov/gmd/ccgg/trends/.

Thai Meteorological Department. 2012. "Annual Weather Summary of Thailand in 2011." 6 February. http://www.tmd.go.th/programs/uploads/ yearlySummary/Annual2011_up.pdf

The Economist. 2011. Disaster Prevention in Brazil. After the Flood. Why did so Many Die? 20 January.

———. 2012. Counting the Cost of Calamities. 14 January. http://www. economist.com/node/21542755.

———. 2015a. As Jokowi Abandons Wasteful Fuel Subsidies, Fiscal Prospects Brighten. 10 January.

———. 2015b. The Biggest Innovation in Energy Is to Go Without. 17 January.

———. 2015c. The Economic Case for Scrapping Fossil Fuel Subsidies Is Getting Stronger. 11 January.

———. 2015d. The Fall in the Price of Oil and Gas Provides a Once-In-A-Generation Opportunity to Fix Bad Energy Policies. 17 January. http://www. economist.com/news/leaders/21639501-fall-price-oil-and-gas-provides-once-generation-opportunity-fix-bad.

The Guardian. 2015. Businesses Still Aren't Feeling Immediately Threatened by Climate Change. 22 January. http://www.theguardian.com/ sustainable-business/2015/jan/22/un-climate-talks-paris-davos-2015-businesses.

Thomas, V., J. R. G. Albert, and C. Hepburn. 2014. "Contributors to the Frequency of Intense Climate Disasters in Asia-Pacific Countries." *Climatic Change* 126 (3–4): 381–98. http://link.springer.com/article/10.1007/ s10584–014–1232-y.

Thomson Reuters. 2014. Global 500 Greenhouse Gas Performance 2010–2013. http://thomsonreuters.com/press-releases/122014/global-500-greenhouse-gas-emissions.

Thorlund, A. C., and G. Potutan. 2015. Bangladesh Forges Ahead on Recovery. United Nations Office for Disaster Risk Reduction News Archive. 19 June. http://www.unisdr.org/archive/44888.

Todd, D., and H. Todd. 2011. *Natural Disaster Response: Lessons from Evaluations of the World Bank.* Worldbank Evaluation Brief 16. Washington, DC: World Bank- Independent Evaluation Group.

Tol, R. S. J. 2011. "The Economic Impact of Climate Change in the 20th and 21st Centuries." *Climate Change* 117 (4): 795–808. http://link.springer. com/article/10.1007%2Fs10584–012–0613–3.

Toya, H., and M. Skidmore. 2007. "Economic Development and the Impacts of Natural Disasters." *Economic Letters* 94 (1): 20–25.

Trenberth, K. E. 2005. "Uncertainty in Hurricanes and Global Warming." *Science* 308:1753–4.

———. 2011. "Changes in Precipitation with Climate Change." *Climate Change Research* 47:123–38. http://www.int-res.com/articles/cr_oa/c047p123.pdf.

United Nations (UN). 2015. *Global Sustainable Development Report: Briefs 2015*. Geneva: United Nations. https://sustainabledevelopment.un.org/content/documents/1870GSDR%202015%20Briefs.pdf

UN Department of Economic and Social Affairs (UNDESA). 2012. Millennium Development Goals Indicators. July. Accessed July 2015. http://mdgs.un.org/unsd/mdg/data.aspx.

UN DESA Population Division. 2012. *World Urbanization Prospects: The 2011 Revision: Highlights.*

———. 2014. *World Urbanization Prospects: The 2014 Revision*. CD-ROM Edition.

UNEP Global Environmental Alert Service (GEAS). 2011. Drought, Fire and Deforestation in the Amazon: Feedbacks, Uncertainty and the Precautionary Approach. UNEP Global Environmental Alert Service. October. http://na.unep.net/geas/newsletter/Oct_11.htm.

———. 2013. Cyclone Phailin in India: Early warning. UNEP Global Environmental Alert Service. November. http://www.unep.org/pdf/UNEP_GEAS_NOV_2013.pdf.

UNEP International Resource Panel. 2014. *Building Natural Capital: How REDD+ can Support a Green Economy*, Report of the International Resource Panel. Nairobi: United Nations Environment Programme.

UNESCAP and United Nations Office for Disaster Risk Reduction (UNISDR). 2010. *Protecting Development Gains: Reducing Disaster Vulnerability and Building Resilience in Asia and the Pacific. The Asia Pacific Disaster Report 2010*. Bangkok: UNESCAP/UNISDR. http://www.unisdr.org/files/16132_asiapacificdisasterreport20101.pdf.

UN Framework Convention on Climate Change (UNFCCC). 2015. Unprecedented Global Breadth of Climate Action Plans Ahead of Paris. UN Climate Change News Room. 2 October. http://newsroom.unfccc.int/unfccc-newsroom/indcs-unprecedented-global-breadth-of-climate-action-plans-ahead-of-paris/.

United Nations Economic and Social Commission for Asia and the Pacific (UNESCAP). 2014. *Statistical Yearbook for Asia and the Pacific 2014*. Bangkok: UNESCAP.

———. 2015. *Disasters in Asia and the Pacific: 2014 Year in Review*. Bangkok: UNESCAP.

United Nations Environment Programme (UNEP). 2014. Lima COP 20/CMP10 UN Climate Conference 2014. Accessed February 2015. http://www.unep.org/climatechange/ClimateChangeConferences/COP20/Highlights/Keyfindingsofforesteconomicvaluations/tabid/794635/Default.aspx.

United Nations Office for Disaster Risk Reduction (UNISDR). 2004. *Living with Risk: A Global Review of Disaster Reduction Initiatives*. Geneva: UNISDR. http://www.unisdr.org/we/inform/publications/657.

———. 2008. Indigenous Knowledge for Disaster Risk Reduction: Good Practices and Lessons Learned from Experiences in the Asia-Pacific Region. http://www.unisdr.org/files/3646_IndigenousKnowledgeDRR.pdf.

———. 2010. Early Warning Practices can Save Many Lives: Good Practices and Lessons Learned. Selected Examples. Bonn: United Nations Secretariat of the International Strategy for Disaster Reduction.

———. 2014. UN Lauds Philippines Handling of Typhoon Hagupit (Ruby). News Archive. 8 December. http://www.unisdr.org/archive/41031.

———. 2015a. *Global Assessment Report on Disaster Risk Reduction 2015. Making Development Sustainable: The Future of Disaster Risk Management.* Geneva: UNISDR.

———. nd. Sendai, Japan: Local Government Profile. *Making Cities Resilient: My City is Getting Ready.* Accessed October 2015. http://www.unisdr.org/campaign/resilientcities/cities/view/1065.

United Nations University-Institute for Environment and Human Security (UNU-EHS). 2014. *World Risk Report 2014.* Bonn: UNU-EHS and Alliance Development Works.

United Nations University-International Human Dimensions Program (UNU-IHDP). 2013. *Inclusive Wealth Report.* New York: Cambridge University Press.

Upton, John. 2013. The India Problem: Why is it Thwarting Every International Agreement? *Slate.* http://www.slate.com/articles/health_and_science/energy_around_the_world/2013/11/india_blocking_climate_talks_warsaw_bangkok_and_ kyoto_negotiations.2.html.

US Energy Information Administration (EIA). International Energy Statistics. http://www.eia.gov/cfapps/ipdbproject/IEDIndex3.cfm?tid=92&pid=46&aid=2 (accessed 13 January 2015).

US Environmental Protection Agency (EPA). 2014. Climate Change. http://www.epa.gov/climatechange/.

Varma, A. 2003. "The Economics of Slash and Burn: A Case Study of the 1997–1998 Indonesian Forest Fires." *Ecological Economics* 46 (1): 159–71. doi:10.1016/S0921-8009(03)00139-3.

Viana, N. 2011. "Floods in Brazil Are a Result of Short Term Planning." *The Guardian,* February.

Webster, P. J., G. J. Holland, J. A. Curry, and H-R. Chang. 2005. "Changes in Tropical Cyclone Number, Duration and Intensity in a Warming Environment." *Science* 309:1844–46. doi:10.1126/science.1116448.

Westra, G. S., L. V. Alexander, and F. W. Zwiers. 2013. "Global Increasing Trends in Annual Maximum Daily Precipitation." *Journal of Climate* 26 (11). doi:http://dx.doi.org/10.1175/JCLI-D-12-00502.1.

White, A. T., P. M. Alino, and A. B. T. Meneses. 2006. "Why Use Marine Protected Areas for Managing Coastal and Marine Habitats and Fisheries?" *Overseas.* 8 (1). http://oneocean.org/overseas/200601/why_use_marine_protected_areas.html.

World Bank. 2003a. *India Andra Pradesh Hazard Mitigation and Emergency Cyclone Recovery Project.* Washington, DC: World Bank.

———. 2003b. *World Development Report 2003: Sustainable Development in a Dynamic World – Transforming Institutions, Growth, and Quality of Life.* doi:https://openknowledge.worldbank.org/handle/10986/5985.

———. 2007a. *Cost of Pollution in The People's Republic of China: Economic Estimates of Physical Damages.* Washington, DC: World Bank. http://documents.worldbank.org/curated/en/2007/02/7503894/cost-pollution-the People's Republic of China-economic-estimates-physical-damages.

———. 2007b. Turkey Marmara Earthquake Emergency Reconstruction Project Implementation, Completion, and Results Report.

———. 2007c. Zambia Emergency Drought Recovery Project PPAR No. 39847. Project Performance Assessment Report.

———. 2009a. *India Gujarat Earthquake Emergency Reconstruction Project.* Washington, DC: World Bank.

———. 2009b. *Sri Lanka: Tsunami Emergency Recovery Program. Implementation, Completion and Results Report.* Washington, DC: World Bank.

———. 2012a. Disaster Risk Management and Multilateral Development Banks: An Overview. Staff Report.

———. 2012b. *Inclusive Green Growth: The Pathway to Sustainable Development.* Washington DC: IBRD/World Bank.

———. 2013. Turn Down the Heat: Climate Extremes, Regional Impacts, and the Case for Resilience. http://documents.worldbank.org/curated/en/2013/06/17862361

———. 2014. Urban Development. http://www.worldbank.org/en/topic/urbandevelopment/.

———. 2015. World Bank, World Development Indicators. January 30. Accessed February 17, 2015. http://databank.worldbank.org/data/views/variableSelection/selectvariables.aspx? source=world-development-indicators#s_e.

World Bank, Asian Development Bank, Japan International Cooperation Agency. 2010. *Climate Risks and Adaptation in Asian Coastal Megacities: A Synthesis Report.* Washington, DC: World Bank. http://documents.worldbank.org/curated/en/2010/09/12886839/climate-risks-adaptation-asian-coastal-megacities-synthesis- report.

World Bank and Global Facility for Disaster Risk Reduction. 2012. *Thai Flood 2011: Rapid Assessment for Resilient Recovery and Reconstruction Planning.* http://www.gfdrr.org/sites/gfdrr/files/publication/Thai_Flood_2011_2.pdf.

World Bank and United Nations. 2010. *Natural Hazards, UnNatural Disasters: the Economics of Effective Prevention.* Washington, DC: World Bank.

World Bank-Independent Evaluation Group. 2006. *Hazards of Nature, Risks to Development: An IEG Evaluation of World Bank Assistance for Natural Disasters.* Washington, DC: World Bank.

———. 2009. *An Evaluation of World Bank Win-Win Energy Policy Reforms (Phase I).* Washington, DC: World Bank. http://hdl.handle.net/10986/2639.

———. 2013. Managing Forest Resources for Sustainable Development. An Evaluation of World Bank Group Experience. http://ieg.worldbank.org/Data/reports/chapters/forest_eval2.pdf.

World Economic Forum. 2015. *Global Risks 2015.* Geneva: World Economic Forum.

World Health Organization (WHO). 2014a. Public health, environmental and social determinants of health. World Health Organization. Accessed February 26, 2015. http://www.who.int/phe/health_topics/outdoorair/databases/cities/en/.

———. 2014b. WHO's Ambient Air Pollution database. Update 2014. World Health Organization.

———. n.d. Media Centre: Climate Change and Health. Accessed December 3, 2016. http://www.who.int/mediacentre/factsheets/fs266/en/.

World Meteorological Organization (WMO). 2006. Statement on Tropical Cyclones and Climate Change. Sixth WMO International Workshop on Tropical Cyclones.

———. 2015. Widespread heatwave affects Europe, Wildfires in North America. 3 July. https://www.wmo.int/media/content/widespread-heatwave-affects-europe-wildfires-north-america.

———. n.d.a. Fast Facts: Tropical Cyclones. Accessed January 13, 2016. http://www.wmo.int/pages/mediacentre/factsheet/tropicalcyclones.html.

———. n.d.b. Natural Hazards. Accessed June 24, 2015. https://www.wmo.int/pages/themes/hazards/index_en.html.

———. n.d. Tropical Cyclones: Question and Answers. Accessed June 24, 2015. https://www.wmo.int/pages/mediacentre/factsheet/tropicalcyclones.html.

Zamzami. 2015. Choked in Smoke – Living in the Thick of Indonesia's Haze. Retrieved from Greenpeace International Blogs September 11. http://www.greenpeace.org/international/en/news/Blogs/makingwaves/Forest-fires-indonesia-pekanbaru/blog/54046/.

Appendix

Appendix Table 1. EM-DAT classification of natural disasters.

Disaster subgroup	Disaster main type	Disaster sub-type	Disaster sub-sub-type
Geophysical: A hazard originating from solid earth. This term is used interchangeably with the term geological hazard.	Earthquake	Ground shaking	
		Tsunami	
	Mass movement		
	Volcanic activity	Ash fall	
		Lahar	
		Pyroclastic flow	
		Lava flow	
Meteorological: A hazard caused by short-lived, micro- to meso-scale extreme weather and atmospheric conditions that last from minutes to days.	Storm	Extra-tropical storm	
		Tropical storm	
		Convective storm	Derecho
			Hail
			Lightning/thunderstorm
			Rain
			Tornado
			Sand/dust storm
			Winter storm/blizzard
			Storm/surge
			Wind
	Extreme temperature	Cold wave	
		Heatwave	
		Severe winter conditions	Snow/ice
			Frost/freeze
	Fog		

(*Continued*)

147

Appendix Table 1. (Continued)

Disaster subgroup	Disaster main type	Disaster sub-type	Disaster sub-sub-type
Hydrological: A hazard caused by the occurrence, movement, and distribution of surface and subsurface freshwater and saltwater.	Flood	Coastal food Riverine flood Flash flood Ice jam flood	
	Landslide	Avalanche (snow, debris, mudflow, rockfall)	
	Wave action	Rogue wave Seiche	
Climatological: A hazard caused by long-lived, meso- to macroscale atmospheric processes ranging from intraseasonal to multidecadal climate variability.	Drought		
	Glacial lake outburst		
	Wildfire	Forest fire Land fire: brush, bush, pasture	

Appendix Table 2. Tropical cyclone formation regions.

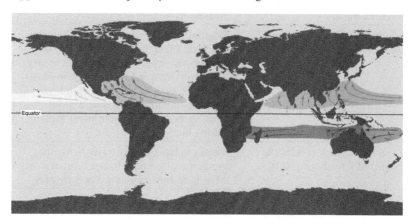

Cyclone basin	Season
Atlantic basin: North Atlantic Ocean, the Gulf of Mexico, and the Caribbean Sea	The hurricane season is "officially" from 1 June to 30 November. Peak activity is in early to mid-September. Once in a few years there may be a tropical cyclone occurring in May or December.
Northeast Pacific basin: Mexico to the international dateline	A broad peak with activity beginning in late May or early June and going until late October or early November, with peak storminess in late August/early September.
Northwest Pacific basin: From the dateline to Asia	Occurs all year round regularly, with a distinct minimum in February and the first half of March. The main season goes from July to November, with a peak in late August/early September.
North Indian basin: Including the Bay of Bengal and the Arabian Sea	A double peak of activity in May and November, though tropical cyclones occur from April to December. Severe cyclonic storms (>74 miles per hour/119 kilometers per hour winds) occur almost exclusively from April to June and again in late September to early December.
Southwest Indian basin: From Africa to about 100°E	Beginning in late October/early November, reaching a double peak in activity: one in mid-January and one in mid-February to early March, and then ending in May.

(*Continued*)

Appendix Table 1. (Continued)

Cyclone basin	Season
Southeast Indian/Australian basin: 100°E to 142°E	Beginning in late October/early November, reaching a double peak in activity: one in mid-January and one in mid-February to early March, and then ending in May. The Australian/Southeast Indian basin February lull in activity is a bit more pronounced than the Southwest Indian basin's lull.
Australian/Southwest Pacific basin:142°E to about 120°W	Begins in late October/early November, reaches a single peak in late February/early March, and then fades out in early May.

Source: NOAA National Weather Service (2011).

Index

Page numbers followed by *b* indicate content in boxes, *f* indicate a figure, and *n* indicate content in notes.

For Product Safety Concerns and Information please contact our EU
representative GPSR@taylorandfrancis.com Taylor & Francis Verlag GmbH,
Kaufingerstraße 24, 80331 München, Germany

Printed and bound by CPI Group (UK) Ltd, Croydon, CR0 4YY
01/05/2025
01858405-0001